Transformation of Higher Education Institutions in Post-Apartheid South Africa

This book outlines successful transformation strategies and efforts that have been developed to assist the South African higher education system in moving beyond its post-apartheid state of being. Through case studies authored by South African higher education scholars and scholars affiliated with South African institutions, this book aims to highlight the status of transformation in the South African higher education system; demonstrate the variety of transformation initiatives used in academic institutions across South Africa; and offer recommendations to further advance this transformation. Written for scholars and advanced students of higher education in international settings, this volume aims to support quality research that benefits the demographic composition of South African academics and students, and offers lessons that can inform higher education transformation in similarly multicultural societies.

Chaunda L. Scott is an associate professor in the Department of Organizational Leadership and Diversity and Inclusion Specialist for the Office of the Dean in the School of Education and Human Services at Oakland University in Rochester, Michigan, USA.

Eunice N. Ivala is an associate professor and coordinator of Educational Technology at the Cape Peninsula University of Technology in Cape Town, South Africa.

T0347954

Transformation of Higher Education Institutions in Post-Apartheid South Africa

Edited by
Chaunda L. Scott and
Eunice N. Ivala

Routledge
Taylor & Francis Group

LONDON AND NEW YORK

First published 2019
by Routledge

2 Park Square, Milton Park, Abingdon, Oxfordshire OX14 4RN
52 Vanderbilt Avenue, New York, NY 10017

Routledge is an imprint of the Taylor & Francis Group, an informa business

First issued in paperback 2020

Library of Congress Cataloguing-in-Publication Data
Names: Scott, Chaunda L., author. | Ivala, Eunice N., author.
Title: Transformation of higher education institutions in
    post-apartheid South Africa / By Chaunda L. Scott and
    Eunice N. Ivala.
Description: New York : Routledge, 2019. | Includes bibliographical
    references and index.
Identifiers: LCCN 2018059218 | ISBN 9781138499782 (hardback) |
    ISBN 9781351014236 (ebook)
Subjects: LCSH: Universities and colleges—South Africa. | Post-
    apartheid era—South Africa. | Educational change—South Africa.
Classification: LCC LA1538 .S36 2019 | DDC 378.68—dc23
LC record available at https://lccn.loc.gov/2018059218

ISBN: 978-1-138-49978-2 (hbk)
ISBN: 978-0-367-67025-2 (pbk)

Typeset in Times New Roman
by Apex CoVantage, LLC

We dedicate this volume to the legacy of Nelson Mandela and to academic faculty in South Africa and globally who cherish the ideals of a democratic free society in which diversity, social justice and social inclusion will be embedded in higher education settings to unify all individuals as they learn and live together with equal opportunities.

Contents

Figures and Tables

Figures

Tables

Foreword

The intense and later violent student protests of 2015–2016 in South African universities left many university leaders with a simple but disturbing realization—that whatever you thought you were doing right was not enough. In fact, you might not even have been doing the right things. For many who think and write about universities there was a period of institutional shock—what on earth is going on? Scholars of higher education scrambled to engage in the difficult task of sense-making on a rare phenomenon.

During the first wave of protests most observers had a fairly comfortable grip on the new reality. Students had left their lecture halls and laboratories to protest their sense of cultural alienation from former White universities. The focus on the giant bronze statue of Cecil John Rhodes at the University of Cape Town (UCT) was simply a convenient and very visible memorial to White power and Black alienation within such institutions. In reality, the grievance was much deeper and the concerns much broader than monuments. What would later be called decolonization was in fact a lament against the lack of Black professors in the academy, the disciplinary curriculum and the paintings that adorned key buildings on campuses. This first wave of protests drew wide public support and presented itself in media images as broadly representative by race and class. All universities responded with an acknowledgment that more needed to be done more visibly and more quickly than before.

By late 2015 and early 2016 the protests had shifted focus from an insistence on decolonization to a demand for free higher education without exception. While government, non-government bodies and well-meaning civic bodies dabbled with a sliding scale for tuition from free education to the poor to some form of co-payment for the middle classes and the wealthy, the core body of protestors demanded free university education for all. Churning in the background was a presidential inquiry into fees which was rendered impotent as the political demands outstripped in pace and fury what many critics saw as nothing more than another delaying tactic all too familiar when government comes under pressure to act.

But the protests also took a darker turn. They had become more violent—campus buildings set alight and destroyed on major campuses—and confrontational but also more stridently racist and sexist across the country. Any attempts at rational debates and invited exchange between university leaders and students were either shut down or strung out to be abandoned near the point of resolution. In response to the assault on both people and property, universities brought additional security onto their campuses. This in turn drew criticism about "the securitization of the universities." University leaders were caught in a bind—how to enable academic freedom and the right to protest, on the one hand, and at the same time provide safety and security to staff and students as well as protect public property. Some universities took the safety and security approach, such as at Wits University, insisting on the rights of non-protestors—by far the majority of students—to study without the violation or disruption of their studies. Others, like UCT, leaned more heavily towards the rights of protestors in a democracy including prolonged occupation of key administrative buildings of the university. UCT sowed great reluctance in acting against violently disruptive students, even inviting participation in a kind of truth and reconciliation process.

What in fact was going on? Such sustained and violent protests were unprecedented on university campuses even during the days of anti-apartheid protest and revolt. The destruction of places of learning and residence was not only unexpected; it was completely new to the experience of universities.

Book-length treatments on the question were generally rushed, unreflective and error-prone. One book openly praised violence and gave "student voice" a paternalistic appearance in its poorly edited chapters. Another was largely descriptive of events without any attempt at going beyond surface features let alone deep theorizing on the meaning of these national protests. Merely rehearsing student demands was hardly serious scholarship. And both academic and general writers wrote as if the problem was one of untransformed campuses that had not moved an inch since 1994. Something deeper in society and on campuses had to be broken for such intense protests to break out two decades into democracy, and for such violent eruptions to happen in places of supposedly higher learning.

In my book entitled: *As by fire* (2017) I tried to grapple with below-the-surface questions about what was really going on in our mere 26 public universities in South Africa. My thesis was that the underlying crisis had to do with the gradual welfarization of universities in recent decades that had reached a point where the expectation of a new generation of students—most from families supported by and with children reared on state grants—was that the government was responsible for their overall welfare including tuition, accommodation and everything else from textbooks to toiletries.

In this context the public university was no different from the local municipality; it was a government office that needed to deliver on the demands of the poor and the needs of "the Black child." If it failed to deliver, the university was subjected to the same treatment as the municipal office—it was the target of violence and on occasion its buildings were burnt down. The university principal was no more than the mayor or the municipal manager. University autonomy was expendable, one of the games leaders play to hold back the government from taking full control of these offices and their resources and distributing them to the poor. University libraries, laboratories and computer center were not vital resources to advance learning but "mere buildings" that can be rebuilt after the storm of protests, like the municipality's property. Universities were places of public employment, not financially vulnerable institutions that could be collapsed with immediate insourcing of contract workers.

In 2015–2016 any illusion of distance between campus and community was dissolved. What was important in this unprecedented level of violent protest was that something more fundamental had changed in the ways in which students and society saw universities. The protests brought about a major culture shift in the perception of universities. Instability was now chronic. Financial vulnerability permanent. Government interference inevitable. What was once restricted to a few universities—many the historically Black universities and universities of technology—was now commonplace in the top research universities like UCT and Witwatersrand.

This does not mean that there will no longer be places called universities or that the ordinary functions of teaching and research or marketing and graduation no longer happened. It means that with chronic instability under conditions of financial and political duress, middle class students will gradually drift away from the leading universities and top professors would be drawn to positions outside of South Africa. Eventually, South Africa's universities would all become poorer and more mediocre, serving an almost exclusively Black student population taught by mainly average academics. In this context the forces re-shaping South African higher education are much more similar to what happened in the post-colonial African university than in the Oxbridge system that birthed the English institutions. That is our fate, unless of course we push back.

It is for this reason that this bold and exciting Focus Book project edited by two prescient scholars of higher education, Drs. Chaunda L. Scott and Eunice N. Ivala, offers a glimmer of hope with respect to the reconstruction of higher education in South Africa. The individual chapters bring to the table vital subjects for analysis and action such as critical citizenship education; transformation and literary texts; digital technologies for unlocking student narratives; flexible learning in elite disciplines like Architecture;

race, diversity and multicultural education in the classroom; research capacity and transformation imperatives, university—industry linkages; and the transformation of universities of technology in the wake of the mergers of more than a decade ago.

These authors, under the guidance of two competent editors, take seriously the issues raised in the 2015–16 protests and give voice to student activists and their issues in the course of doing their work from academic development to research supervision to community development. The editors skillfully bring into the conversation issues of policy, politics, programming and practice in addressing what I have called the transformation imperatives in South African universities. In the process they bring a whole new generation of young scholars into active reflection and publication in the field of higher education.

This book could simply not have come at a more important time in our history.

Dr. Jonathan D. Jansen
2016–17 Fellow, Center for Advanced Study in the
Behavioral Sciences
Stanford University, USA

Former Vice Chancellor and Professor
University of the Free State
Bloemfontein, South Africa

Preface

Over the past two decades, much has been written on the topic of transforming the South African Higher Education System. Yet, research remains scant regarding what successful transformation strategies have been utilized and needed to move South Africa's higher education system beyond its post-apartheid state of being from the perspective of South African academic faculty. This Focus Book gives voice to South African academic faculty members representing different universities across the Republic of South Africa, who are transformation agents in South Africa's higher education system, for the purpose of informing global scholars about the kinds of successful strategies they believe are currently being utilized to further transform South Africa's higher education system, as well as learn what strategies they believe are needed. The information in this volume will be useful to scholars globally that are interested in issues of reconstruction, governance, policy, curriculum development, diversity education and learning, and social inclusion as it relates to transforming the South African higher education system beyond its current post-apartheid state of being.

Chapter 1, the introduction chapter, will begin by presenting a concise summary of the impact apartheid and the current post-apartheid state of being have had on South Africa's higher education system. In the next section of this chapter, benchmarks established by the Republic of South Africa that have and presently serve to guide the process of transformation in higher education and training institutions in post-apartheid South Africa will be introduced and discussed. These benchmarks are: *The Education White Paper 3: A Programme for the Transformation of Higher Education* (Department of Education, 1997), *Transformation and Restructuring: A New Institutional Landscape for Higher Education* (Ministry of Education, 2002) and most recently the *Policy Framework for the Realization of Social Inclusion in the Post School Education and Training System* (Minister of Education (2016). Therefore, this chapter serves to provide the context for the scholarly writings that follow.

Chapter 2 presents a pragmatic case study of ten lecturers' reflections on the utilization of Curricular Spider Web (CSW) in teaching and supervising Master of Education (MEd) students. The lecturers were involved in the teaching/supervision of MEd Curriculum Development students. The purpose of the chapter is to explore the lecturers' reflections on the utilization of CSW in teaching. This chapter consequently recommends and demonstrates how the diagonal/personal reflections frames both the vertical and horizontal reflections to produce reflective graduates with knowledge, skills and values/ attitudes required for local, national and international activities.

Chapter 3 argues that the current language and academic literacies strategy at the University of Johannesburg (UJ) seems not only fragmented in its approaches but also overwhelming vis-à-vis the students' level of competence and their ability to overcome their own deficit. This chapter will present the status quo of language and academic literacies at the University of Johannesburg and will contextualize possible pragmatic academic and language literacies solutions.

Chapter 4 discusses that while numerous higher education policies have been adopted in South Africa over the past two decades, more platforms need to be created to attract previously excluded groups, particularly Black women, from a range of social contexts. This chapter presents a descriptive analysis of the lived experiences and career development of Black female novice academics in a selected South African higher education institution. It draws on critical consciousness theory and an asset-based framework to highlight their voices as critical assets in strengthening the transformation of higher education. The findings indicate that a collective transformative journey creates a safe space and a supportive learning environment to reflect on "the novice's" views and practices while fostering active agency in advancing transformation as individuals and as a collective.

Chapter 5 reports on a case study involving student teachers of literature in a teacher education programme who used literary texts as catalysts for implementing transformation. While the requirements of the degree asserted sound disciplinary knowledge and effective pedagogical skills, there was an unrecognized need for an understanding of how to bring about academic and social transformation in the school classrooms in which these students would work, irrespective of context or resources. The study was guided by the following question: What strategies may be used in a teacher education lecture room in South Africa to empower student teachers with the knowledge, skills and abilities to bring about academic and social transformation and contribute successfully to the educational context within and beyond the classroom?

In Chapter 6 the authors reflect on the key issues at play related to novice supervisors in the higher education postgraduate supervision context in South

Africa. The author draws on evidence from having taught on a structured, funded research supervision capacity-building programme at eight higher education institutions in South Africa over the past four years (2015–2018). While each university context and cohort of students was uniquely different and presented with parochial issues, there were certain universal postgraduate supervision challenges, dilemmas, opportunities and constraints that were common across all institutions. This chapter focuses on an analysis of the most pertinent issues at play with a view to theorizing their occurrence and offering tentative insights to engage these issues.

Chapter 7 relies on Critical Theory as both a conceptual and analytical framework to examine the strategic organizational development initiatives of the Durban University of Technology (DUT), with reference to the current and future role of the university's academic development division in advancing the institution's social justice agenda as articulated in its current strategic plan. In a theory-informed discussion of academic development (also termed "educational development" in some parts of the world), the chapter locates the vision and goals of the DUT academic development division—known as the Centre for Excellence in Learning and Teaching (CELT)—in the broader context of academic development both in South Africa and globally.

Chapter 8 explores inclusivity in South African higher education academic practices for previously marginalized groups, which is still in an exploratory phase, despite an increase in South African higher education transformation research. There are many challenges that present barriers to bringing about meaningful transformation, one of which could be the lack of some type of inclusivity framework. This chapter attempts to address the problem of how to promote marginalized-group inclusivity by borrowing from theories of academic professional identity formation and inclusivity, to analyze accounts of lived experiences of Black women academics from marginalized groups in one South African university located in the Eastern Cape. This chapter provides a preview of how this information could be used to develop an inclusivity framework for Black women academics in South African institutions.

Chapter 9 examines practices or initiatives that would be beneficial in further advancing transformation in universities. While transformation in South Africa has broadly been viewed as a process of redressing the apartheid past through racial and gender dynamics, this chapter focuses on the role of the university in transformation in terms of students' teaching and learning experiences. Drawing on selected post-apartheid higher education policies and the response by the University of KwaZulu-Natal (UKZN), this chapter shows the varied efforts to transform universities in South Africa, as well as the need for the epistemological dimensions in teaching and learning to be complemented by ontological dimensions in furthering transformation.

References

Department of Education. (1997, July). *Education white paper 3: A programme for the transformation of higher education. Pretoria, South Africa.* Retrieved from www.gov.za/sites/www.gov.za/files/18207_gen1196_0.pdf

Minister of Education. (2002, June). *Transformation and restructuring: A new institutional landscape for higher education.* Retrieved from www.dhet.gov.za/Reports%20Doc%20Library/New%20Institutional%20landscape%20for%20Higher%20Education%20in%20South%20Africa.pdf

Minister of Education. (2016, December). *Policy framework for the realization of social inclusion in the post school education and training system.* Retrieved from www.dhet.gov.za/SiteAssets/Latest%20News/2017/January/Gazetted-Policy-Framework-for-the-Realisation-of-Social-Inclusion-in-PSET-No40496-Notice-no-1560.pdf

Acknowledgments

This Focus Book would not have been possible without Matthew Friberg, Education Editor for Routledge Publishers and the Routledge Publishers Education unit, who provided us with the opportunity to have this volume published. We want to thank Routledge Editors Sharon Golan and Karen Adler for their support of this book project and for putting us in contact with Matthew Friberg. We are grateful for the collective scholarly efforts of South African faculty members and faculty members from the United States who served as chapter authors and reviewers for this book project. Moreover, we applaud the colleagues previously mentioned who are involved in theory and or practice in helping to transform South Africa's higher education system beyond its post-apartheid state of being. I, Dr. Eunice N. Ivala, am thankful to Dr. Chaunda L. Scott, who came up with the idea for this Focus Book project when she was a Fulbright Specialist Scholar in 2015 at Cape Peninsula of Technology in Cape Town, South Africa, and for leading this book project to fruition. We are also grateful to Dr. Jonathan D. Jansen for his support and for writing the foreword for this volume. Last but least, we want to thank our colleagues, family members and friends who provided us with ongoing encouragement which helped to make this critical Focus Book a reality.

1 Moving From Apartheid to a Post-Apartheid State of Being and Its Impact on Transforming Higher Education Institutions in South Africa

Chaunda L. Scott and Eunice N. Ivala

> *"No country can really develop unless its citizens are educated."*
> *Nelson Mandela (The Borgen Project, 2018)*

Introduction

Over the past two decades, much has been written on the topic of transforming the South African higher education (HE) system. Yet, research from the perspective of South African academic staff members representing a variety of universities remains scant regarding what transformation strategies have been successful, unsuccessful or needed to move South Africa's (SA) HE system beyond its post-apartheid state of being. This chapter begins by presenting a brief summary of the impact apartheid and the current post-apartheid state of being have had on SA's HE system. In the next section of this chapter, benchmarks established by the Republic of SA that have and presently serve to guide the process of transformation in HE and training institutions in post-apartheid SA will be introduced and discussed. These benchmarks are: *The Education White Paper 3: A Programme for the Transformation of Higher Education* (Department of Education, 1997), *Transformation and Restructuring: A New Institutional Landscape for Higher Education* (Ministry of Education, 2002) and most recently the *Policy Framework for the Realization of Social Inclusion in the Post School Education and Training System* (Minister of Higher Education and Training, 2016). The insights from this chapter serve to provide the context of the scholarly writings that follow.

This Focus Book entitled: *Transformation of Higher Education Institutions in Post-Apartheid South Africa* is a result of a research collaboration Dr. Chaunda L. Scott led as a Fulbright Specialist Scholar in the Republic of SA. In 2015, Dr. Scott received a prestigious Fulbright Specialist Scholar award at Cape Peninsula University of Technology (CPUT) located in Cape Town, South Africa, the only University of Technology in the province, and the largest university in the Western Cape in terms of student enrollments. As a Fulbright Specialist Scholar at CPUT, Dr. Scott had an awesome opportunity as an Associate Professor of Organizational Leadership and Diversity and Inclusion Specialist in the School of Education and Human Services at Oakland University located in Rochester, Michigan, USA, to provide diversity education workshops to academic faculty and staff members at the Fundani Centre for Higher Education Development and to engage in diversity education research. She also had an opportunity to learn directly from CPUT academic faculty about the impact apartheid had on SA and its HE system during 1948–1994, as well as presently, and witness the #FeesMustFall student demonstrations in Cape Town in 2015.

The products that were produced from the diversity education research that Dr. Scott engaged in with Dr. Eunice N. Ivala, Associate Professor and Coordinator Educational Technology at CPUT, resulted in two Routledge Publishers Focus Books, of which this volume is one. The second Focus Book is entitled: *Faculty Perspectives on Transformation of Vocational Training in Post-Apartheid South Africa: Lessons and Innovations from Cape Peninsula University of Technology*. The aim of these two publications is to provide an opportunity for South African academic faculty members representing various universities throughout SA to share their perspectives on the current status of HE in post-apartheid SA.

In the next sections of this chapter, a brief background will be presented on the impact apartheid and the current post-apartheid state of being have had on SA's HE system. To conclude this chapter, three important benchmarks will be summarized that were established by the Republic of SA's HE system after apartheid ended in 1994 to address past inequities and transform SA's HE and training system in regard to serving all learners in their new democratic society. These benchmarks are entitled: *White Paper 3: A Programme for the Transformation of Higher Education* (Department of Education, 1997), *Transformation, Restructuring: A New Institutional Landscape for Higher Education* (Ministry of Education, 2002), and most recently the *Policy Framework for the Realization of Social Inclusion in the Post School Education and Training System* (Minister of Higher Education and Training, 2016). Thus, the information presented in this chapter serves to provide the context for the chapters that follow.

Apartheid and Post-Apartheid Education System

Apartheid in SA 1948–1994, can be defined as a legal policy or system that separated and discriminated against individuals based solely on racial line. In 1948, the Apartheid legal system was established in SA by an all-White political party that gained political power for the purpose of separating White

South Africans from other races or more specifically, from Asians, Indians, Colored individuals (mixed race individuals) and Black South Africans, who then and now, make up the majority of the population in SA. Apartheid was also created to divide and rule Black South Africans by tribes in order to lessen their political influence and power (Apartheid, 2018).

Under the apartheid laws, non-White South Africans were treated reprehensibly according to their racial background (A History of Apartheid in South Africa, 2018). For example, non-White South Africans during the apartheid years were not allowed to own land, vote, marry outside of their race and utilize public facilities reserved for Whites only. Such facilities included: restaurants, restrooms, drinking fountains, benches, including public and private schools. Non-White South Africans also had to live in restricted areas and carry passes to be in areas designated for White South Africans. Non-White South Africans were as well deprived of the opportunity to take part in political affairs (Apartheid, 2018). In the area of education during the apartheid years, the Bantu Act was created and run by the South African Government in 1953 (South Africa: Overcoming Apartheid Build Democracy, 2018). The purpose of the Bantu Act was to prevent Black South Africans from receiving the same educational opportunities afforded to White South Africans (Hartshorne, 1992). Moreover, the Bantu Act aimed to keep the Black South African students from concentrating on the poor quality of education that they were receiving in these schools (South Africa: Overcoming Apartheid Build Democracy, 2018).

From the mid 1950's through the mid 1980's, public acts of disapproval towards apartheid were exhibited throughout SA in the forms of: non-violent demonstrations, marches, student protests and political protests, to name a few (Apartheid, 2018). By the late 1980's, the South African government was being pressured by the international community to end apartheid and in 1989, apartheid laws were also being dismantled. In 1994, apartheid ended when non-White voters unanimously elected Nelson Mandela as their new president (Apartheid, 2018).

By the late 1990's, the present SA's HE system began creating benchmarks (which will be summarized later in this chapter) to guide South African higher education institutions (HEIs) in responding to the new realities of transforming past apartheid policies and practices, while educating and servicing a diverse population of students simultaneously. Over the past two decades, SA's HE system has made important gains in transforming their HE and training system. For instance, some of these gains include: increased non-White student enrollments, especially Black South African enrollments and graduation success rates in universities across SA (Macha & Kadakia, 2017). Moreover, according to MacGregor (2014) the South African government has allocated more funding to its HE and training system. Most recently, research and post-graduate education have increased in the areas of science and knowledge production, and in 2017, the president of SA, Jacob Zuma, publicized that free HE tuition would be given to first year college students that are from families making less than $25,000.00 a year (Muller, 2018).

While these achievements in the post-apartheid SA HE and training system are significant, ongoing transformation efforts are needed to move the SA HE and training system beyond its post- apartheid state of being. For example, the rise in low income students of color, specifically Black South African students on university campuses throughout SA, along with the rise of university student protests on these campuses throughout SA in the 21st century, makes it clear that there is a need for: 1) free and lower tuition fees; 2) first generation pre-college student preparation programmes to assist these students in achieving graduation success; 3) diverse administrators, academic faculty and staff members to reflect the student population they are now serving; 4) new and updated infrastructures; 5) updated facilities; 6) new academic and student support services and programmes; 7) new technological equipment, such as computers and projectors, along with; 8) funding to support universities in SA in achieving benchmark standards established by the South African department of Higher Education and Training (DHET) in collaboration with the Department of Education (DOE).

Transformation Policy Frameworks for Post-Apartheid Higher Education in South Africa

1. The Education White Paper 3: A Programme for the Transformation of Higher Education

Over 20 years as a democracy, SA is still redressing past inequalities and efforts are made to transform the HE system to serve a new social order, to meet pressing national needs and to respond to new realities and opportunities. The former DOE released the *Education White Paper 3: A Programme of Transformation for Higher Education*, July 1997. This white paper outlines a comprehensive set of initiatives for the transformation of HE through the development of a single coordinated system with new planning, governing and funding arrangements. As stated in the white paper, all higher education institutions (HEIs) should implement these initiatives in their work. In this white paper, transformation of HE is described as: eradication of all forms of discrimination; promotion of equity of access and fair chances of success for all; advancement of redress of inequalities; meeting, through its teaching, learning and research programmes, national development needs, including the economy's high skilled employment needs; supporting democratic ethos and a culture of human rights through education programmes and practices conducive to critical discourse and creative thinking, cultural tolerance and a commitment to a humane, non-racist and non-sexist social order; and contributing to the advancement of all forms of knowledge and scholarship and upholding rigorous standards of academic quality.

2. Transformation and Restructuring: A New Institutional Landscape for Higher Education

After the democratic election in 1994, it became evident that there was a need for a new democratic education system which ensured equality in all aspects of education (Sayed, 2000). According to Makgoba (2008, p. 1), the new government inherited "a HE system whereby the leadership was unable to provide the vision needed to meet the knowledge and scholarship challenges of HE in the context of national transformation, globalization and a development state . . . the sector suffered an identity crisis, the effects of poor human capital production levels, fragmentation along race lines, a lack of sustainability and a structural incapacity to meet the rigorous challenges of reconstruction and development." Structurally, fundamental and long standing problems existed, which included the geographical location of institutions which was based on ideological and political considerations rather than rational and coherent planning. This resulted in fragmentation and unnecessary duplication and the continued and increasing fragmentation of the system. Education did not work in a coordinated way—there were limited successful co-operative initiatives and programmes between institutions; major inefficiencies related to student throughput rates (low throughput rates), graduation (low graduation rates), student dropouts (a large number of students dropout), student repetition and the retention of failing students and unit costs across the system; skewed patterns of distribution of students in the various fields of study: Science, Engineering and Technology (SET), Business and Commerce, and the Humanities and Education, with greater concentration of students in the humanities and education field relative to other fields; the distribution of students in the various levels and fields of study at certain institutions was skewed in terms of race and gender; academic and administrative staff (in many fields and disciplines and at different levels) also displayed poor patterns of race and gender representation and distribution; and most institutions had extremely low research outputs and even those institutions with a higher ratio of research outputs relative to other institutions had uneven levels of outputs (CHE Shape and Size Task Team, 2000). These structural characteristics undermined cost-effectiveness, efficiency and equity. They created a kind of differentiation that is neither desirable, sustainable nor equitable in a developing democracy.

The post-apartheid HE institutions were also faced with immediate or contextual problems which included: institutional responses that exacerbated the inherited fragmentation and incoherence of the system and the inefficient and ineffective utilization of resources; competition between public institutions around programme offerings and student enrollments, which overshadowed cooperation and lead towards homogeneity and sameness in an environment of declining enrollment; the decline in student enrollments within the public HE sector compounded by a decline in retention rate of students from the first to succeeding years of study and the overall participation rate for the age group 20–14 remained static and was estimated for 1999 at 15%; the possible inability of several institutions to continue to fund their activities because of the relationship between enrollments and funding as well as their inability to attract more diverse sources of funding and the inability of many students to pay fees, as well as the institutions' lack of capacity to collect fees and resulting increases in students' debts; concerns around quality, the effective protection of learners and possible adverse effects on the public HE systems by the increase in private HEIs who were at that time inadequately regulated in terms of registration, accreditation and quality assurance; fragile governance capacity (council, management, administration and students) in many of the institutions; inadequate senior and middle management capacities within the system; the rapid incorporation of information and communication technologies within HE; and the inadequate information systems, especially in relation to finance matters. As a result, many institutions lacked the capacity to provide and process basic data and information (CHE Shape and Size Task Team, 2000).

As a result of the above challenges, the inherited HE system was not effectively responding to the new needs of the country and there was a need to restructure the HE system. In December 2002, the then minister of Education, Professor Kader Asmal, announced that the cabinet had approved the final proposal for the restructuring of the institutional landscape of HE in SA. The restructuring of HE was in line with the Constitution of SA, which emphasizes the new democratic government's commitment to restoring the human rights of all marginalized groups; the bill of rights, which entrenches the rights of all South Africans to basic education and access to educational institutions regardless of race, gender, sexual orientation, disability, religion, culture or language (RSA, 1996); the National Plan for Higher Education (2001) (Ministry of Education, 2001) stressed the need to ensure the "fitness for purpose" of the South African HE system (Makgoba, 2008); and the *White Paper 3: A Programme for the Transformation of Higher Education*, advanced equity and redress, quality, development, effectiveness and efficiency (CHE Shape and Size Task Team, 2000).

The overall objective of the restructuring of the HE landscape was the development of a HE system that delivers effectively and efficiently and is based on equity, quality and excellence; responsiveness; and good governance and management (CHE Shape and Size Task Team, 2000). The White Paper 3 called for a coherent, coordinated and integrated national HE system that is simultaneously differentiated and characterized by diversity. Differentiation was used to refer to the social and educational mandates of institutions and diversity was used with reference to the specific institutional missions—which were said should be varied. The purpose of differentiation and diversity was to ensure a range of institutions, institutional programmes and capabilities appropriate to national needs.

The envisaged outcomes of the restructuring were: a much more clearly specified range of institutional mandates that encouraged diversity through explicit, clear and coherent institution-specific missions in their pursuit of production of knowledge and graduates; a clearer and more targeted set of objectives for the investment of resources to strengthen quality and equity; a prospect of increasing overall participation levels in HE and ways of addressing the challenge of equity of access; a more focused framework for innovation in teaching and learning, research and in community service through a concentration of resources and attention on niche areas; provision for and encouragement of different modes of teaching, learning and assessment and establishment of possibilities and limitations of different modes of delivery for different institutional focuses; and acknowledgment of a framework for competition as well as collaboration, within the public sector as well as between the public and the private HE providers, as competition within a properly regulated system enhances quality (CHE Shape and Size Task Team, 2000).

As a result of the restructuring process, the number of universities in SA were cut from 36 to 23 through incorporations and mergers. However, the government in 2014–2015 has established 3 more universities to bring the total of public universities to 26. Public universities in SA are divided into three types: traditional universities, which offer theoretically oriented university degrees; universities of technology ("technikons"), which offer vocational oriented certificates, diplomas and degrees; and comprehensive universities, which offer a combination of both types of qualification. Thus, the country has 9 universities of technology; 6 comprehensive universities; and 11 traditional universities. These universities accommodate in excess of 1 million students, with plans by government to add 500,000 to that total by 2030.[1]

3. The Policy Framework for the Realization of Social Inclusion in the Post-School Education and Training System

The policy framework was developed in 2016 in an effort to understand social inclusion in the Post-School Education and Training (PSET) system and to ensure the implementation of social inclusion in all forms of PSET institutions (public universities, HE colleges, university colleges, Technical and Vocational Education and Training (TVET) colleges and private universities). Additionally, the policy is intended to help the DHET, and HE and training institutions, in implementing and reporting on elements of social inclusion. Furthermore, the policy will assist DHET in ensuring that the transformation priorities of the Department are taken into account at all PSET institutions. The framework will also assist DHET in: strengthening relationships with other government departments dealing with issues of social cohesion; ensuring that there is synergy and shared understanding as far as the implementation of social inclusion is concerned; and addressing a major challenge facing the (PSET) system—the lack of an integrated framework defining the roadmap to a socially inclusive PSET system that is in line with the values of the South African Constitution.

The framework situates the PSET system within the universal human rights discourse, which recognizes social inclusion as a concept which embraces the entire humanity and cuts across all the factors that divide human beings. In this discourse, social cohesion is said to recognize the fact that all human beings, regardless of national boundaries of states, socio-economic background, age, disability, ethnic or racial origin, religion and any other form of belief are entitled to human dignity and should be protected by the State. Thus, the policy framework was developed in alignment with: The Universal Declaration of Human Rights proclaimed by the United Nations General Assembly in Paris on 10 December 1948 (General Assembly resolution 217 A), which sets a common standard of achievements for all peoples and all nations. The Universal Declaration of Human Rights spells out, for the first time, that fundamental human rights should be universally acknowledged and protected. In its preamble, it recognizes the inherent dignity and the equal and inalienable rights of all people as the foundation of freedom, justice and peace in the world; the South African Bill of Rights is embedded in the Constitution of the Republic of SA (RSA, 1996). The bill of rights acknowledges the rights of all people in SA and affirms the democratic values of human dignity, equality and freedom. The policy framework recognizes the values underpinned in the preamble of the Constitution and which are also restated in the Manifesto on Values, Education and Democracy, as published by the DOE in 2001.

The policy framework complements other DHET and various government departments' existing policies and legislation that address social inclusion issues in PSET (DHET, 2016). The DHET hopes to create an environment that will ensure that social inclusion-related policies and legislation in institutions are developed, implemented and monitored. The DHET and institutions reporting to it are expected to align their implementation strategies and long-term plans with international conventions and declarations. In this regard, the DHET is obliged to contribute to periodical country reports and work collaboratively with other departments addressing issues of social inclusion.

Even though a lot has been achieved in attaining social inclusion in SA, including the instituting of a solid policy and legislative environment, major challenges still exist. The Ministerial Report on Transformation and Social Cohesion and the Elimination of Discrimination in SA's Public HEIs (2009) revealed that there was still racism and other forms of discrimination in South African public HEIs. Other challenges identified were lack of transformation in areas such as gender, disability and representation of other racial groups in academic positions. The report also highlighted the need to promote diversity not only in the student population but also to ensure that the academic staff composition is equally diverse and institutional cultures of exclusion are transformed. The reports additionally showed that HEIs do not have a shared understanding of "transformation" and "social cohesion."

In order to realize social inclusion in the PSET system, the policy framework states five strategic themes: eradication of poverty and social exclusion in the system by mobilization of all PSET institutions and stakeholders in the sector towards common social inclusion objectives; common indicators to measure progress in the achievement of social inclusion; the development of evidence based progress reports indicating performance against national action plans on social inclusion; mutual learning and exchange on social inclusion in the PSET system; and social inclusion assessment in the form of annual reports on progress of social inclusion in PSET.

According to the policy frameworks, for the PSET system to work towards achieving social inclusion, institutions should focus on:

- Governance—governing structures of institutions should be representative; freedom of association and freedom of expression as articulated in Chapter 2 of the Constitution should be observed; and training of council members in social inclusion dimensions is critical as these structures are crucial in the development and implementation of progressive institutional policies.
- Democratic representation of staff and students—democratic representation for both staff and students cannot be divorced from the broader debate of social inclusion, access and transformation. The policy framework supports staff development, creation of posts and mentorship as part of institutional plans and departmental initiatives such as the new Generation of Academics Programme (nGAP), which encompasses both historically advantaged and disadvantaged HEs. It further suggests that institutions should have clear transformation supporting policies and guidelines with regard to teaching and learning, staff promotion and clear indicators for teaching, learning and research. Additionally,

University councils should establish functional employment equity processes and procedures and monitor and report on employment equity trends in terms of the Employment Equity Act and employment equity should be part of the Vice-Chancellors' employment contracts.

- Improving access to previously disadvantaged students—government aims at addressing financial support for students in institutions through increased National Student Financial Aid Scheme (NSFAS) financial allocations and new management systems, as well as the recent focus on the "missing middle" (refers to students above NSFAS threshold but for whom university education is unaffordable), as most Black students entering HE come from poor and middle class households.
- Addressing the needs of students and staff with disabilities—the framework supports the Ministerial Statements on Disability Funding and the norm that all infrastructural programmes have to address disability issues. It notes that most universities have progressed significantly in developing disability units, building needed infrastructure to support staff and students with disabilities and implementing disability policies.
- Dialogue forums—establishment of dialogue forums should be encouraged and supported in institutions as they nurture a culture of debate and democratic participation in public affairs.
- Gender equity—according to The Human Sciences Research Council (HSRC) policy brief (July 2014), the quality of educational experiences for both male and female students remains poor in SA, and thus, there was a need for priority assistance for women in the PSET system. This assistance must be formalized in institutional policies and should be grounded on applicable national legislation. Gender equity policies and targets should be put in place in all institutions and be part of PSET institutions' transformation reports, and targets should not be limited to the number of women admitted as students or employed by institutions, but also address their occupation of leadership positions, participation in post-graduate studies, as well as their participation and success rate in previously male-dominated programmes such as engineering and political sciences.
- Healthcare and HIV/AIDS—institutions must prioritize establishment of health centers and student support services, in order to promote healthy lifestyle on and off campus, assist staff and students in health-related issues and in specific conduct an HIV and AIDS information and awareness campaign.
- Student accommodation—institutions should have placement policies that will be centrally monitored by the residence office of each institution and the framework pleas for the abolition of any form of racial segregation and discrimination in student residences. The policy calls

for the banning of initiation ceremonies and activities, "irrespective of whether an activity causes bodily harm or not," as these activities and ceremonies could be used as a cover to promote racial bigotry in institutions and thus threaten social cohesion. It further calls for institutional employment equity policies to be applied to residence employees in order to avoid the perpetuation of ethnic or racial composition of residence staff.

With the understanding that: social inclusion and transformation cannot be separated; government fiscal budget constraints and the recommendation that integrated planning and implementation within current budgets will need to be used to attain the goals of this policy framework; the fact that social inclusion implementation in institutions was to begin in 2018–2019; absence of DHET monitoring and an evaluation report on social inclusion (as the policy states that this evaluation will be done in 2019–2020); the fact that HEIs do not have a shared understanding of transformation and social inclusion; and the acknowledgment that implementation of transformation and social inclusion will not be the same for all institutional types, the subsequent chapters present efforts of some of the universities of technology, traditional and comprehensive universities towards transformation and social inclusion.

Note

1 https://businesstech.co.za/news/general/101412/here-are-south-africas-26-univer
sities/

References

Apartheid. (2018). *Apartheid*. Retrieved from www.history.com/topics/apartheid
The Borgen Project. (2018). *Top nine Nelson Mandela quotes about education*. Retrieved from https://borgenproject.org/nelson-mandela-quotes-about-education/
Council on Higher Education Size and Shape Task Team. (2000). *Towards a higher education Landscape: Meeting the equity, quality and social development imperatives of South Africa in the 21st century*. Pretoria: Council on Higher Education.
Department of Education. (1997, July). *Education white paper 3: A programme for the transformation of higher education*. Pretoria, South Africa. Retrieved from www.gov.za/sites/www.gov.za/files/18207_gen1196_0.pdf
Department of Higher Education and Training. (2016). *Policy Framework for the Realization of Social Inclusion in the Post-School Education and Training System*. Retrieved from http://www.dhet.gov.za/SiteAssets/Latest%20News/2017/January/Gazetted-Policy-Framework-for-the-Realisation-of-Social-Inclusion-in-PSET-No 40496-Notice-no-1560.pdf

Hartshorne, K. (1992). *Crisis and challenge: Black education 1910–1990.* Cape Town: Oxford University Press. Retrieved from https://www.cia.gov/library/publications/the-world-factbook/print/bc.html.

A History of Apartheid in South Africa. (2018). Retrieved from www.sahistory.org.za/article/history-apartheid-south-africa

MacGregor, K. (2014). Higher education in the 20th year of democracy. *University World News.* Retrieved from www.universityworldnews.com/article.php?story=20140425131554856

Macha, W., & Kadakia, A. (2017). *Education systems profile.* Education in South Africa. WENR World Education + News Review. Retrieved from https://wenr.wes.org/2017/05/education-south-africa

Makgoba, M. W. (2008). In practice: Engaging with leaders in higher education. *Leadership Foundation for Higher Education,* (16). Retrieved from http://ifhe.ac.uk

Ministry of Education. (2001). *Draft National Plan for Higher Education In South Africa.* Retrieved from http://www.dhet.gov.za/HED%20Policies/National%20Plan%20on%20Higher%20Education.pdf

Minister of Education. (2002). *Transformation and restructuring a new institutional landscape from higher education.* Retrieved from www.dhet.gov.za/Reports%20Doc%20Library/New%20Institutional%20landscape%20for%20Higher%20Education%20in%20South%20Africa.pdf

Minister of Higher Education and Training. (2016). *Policy framework for the realization of social inclusion in the post school education and training system.* Retrieved from www.dhet.gov.za/SiteAssets/Latest%20News/2017/January/Gazetted-Policy-Framework-for-the-Realisation-of-Social-Inclusion-in-PSET-No40496-Notice-no-1560.pdf

Muller, S. (2018). Free higher education South Africa: Cutting through the lies and statistics. *The Conversation.* Retrieved from https://theconversation.com/free-higher-education-in-south-africa-cutting-through-the-lies-and-statistics-90474

Republic of South Africa. (1996). *Constitution of the republic of South Africa.* Pretoria: Government Printer.

Sayed, Y. (2000). *Post-apartheid educational transformation: Policy concerns and approaches.* Paper presented at EAKA Conference, New Orleans.

South Africa: Overcoming Apartheid Building Democracy. (2018). *Bantu education.* Retrieved from http://overcomingapartheid.msu.edu/sidebar.php?id=65-258-2

Theme 1

Producing Successful Graduates

What strategies are being utilized or could be utilized in institutions of higher learning in South Africa to produce graduates at the undergraduate, master's and doctorate levels with the knowledge, skills and abilities to contribute successfully in the industry, the community and globally?

2 Lecturers' Reflections on Curricular Spider Web Concepts as Transformation Strategies

Simon Bhekimuzi Khoza

Introduction

A study conducted by Dewey (1933) on teachers' reflections defined reflection as an interrogation of beliefs from various forms of knowledge, based on evidence, in order to make life decisions. Reflections are being utilized by higher education institutions (HEIs) as curriculum transformation strategies (Khoza, 2017). When lecturers reflect on their teaching, they face the tension between the vertical (market-driven/professional) curriculum and horizontal (societal-driven/social) curriculum (Khoza, 2018; le Grange, 2016). This suggests that lecturers reflect-on-teaching (vertical) and/or reflect-in-learning (horizontal) (Schön, 1983). On the one hand, reflections have been driven by a constructivism learning theory (horizontal) that aims at building a society/community of practice (Amory, 2012; Badat, 2010). The horizontal curriculum favors students over lecturers. Students like socialization, and are perceived to be "digital natives," "screenagers," or "clickerati" (Prensky, 2001; Rushkof, 2006); while lecturers like curriculum rules and are perceived as digital immigrants or refugees (Khoza & Manik, 2015). In other words, students enjoy digital technology for socialization because they were born within the technology environment, while lecturers learn digital technology as their new experiences. On the other hand, HEIs have content (vertical) to be taught by lecturers and mastered by students, in order to pass their qualification (Hoadley & Jansen, 2014). The vertical curriculum favors lecturers more than students, because they publish content through journals, books and other sources. However, studies on reflections had not identified curriculum concepts for reflections, until a study conducted by Van den Akker (2003) and supported by Khoza (2018) framed the curriculum concepts as the Curricular Spider Web (CSW). As a result, when lecturers reflect they directly/indirectly use the CSW, to produce the reflection-on-teaching (vertical-content driven) and/or reflection-in-learning (horizontal-outcomes driven) (Govender & Khoza, 2017; Khoza & Manik, 2015).

Therefore, these differences in reflections suggest a need for a new curriculum based on the two reflections, which may harmonize the two types of curriculum reflections into one strong unit. This chapter argues for a pragmatic (diagonal) curriculum for reflection, which may unite the horizontal curriculum with the vertical curriculum, thus helping HEIs to overcome the tension between these two curricula. Studies strongly suggest reflections as a solution to any tension caused by the two approaches in education (Dewey, 1933; Maxwell, 2013; Schön, 1983; Van Manen, 1977).

Thus this chapter presents a pragmatic case study of 10 lecturers' reflections on the utilization of Curricular Spider Web (CSW) in teaching and supervising Master of Education (MEd) students.

Curriculum Reflections

Curriculum as a plan for teaching and learning (Berkvens, van den Akker, & Brugman, 2014) and as a plan of teaching and learning (Pinar, 2012) is driven by CSW concepts (Table 2.1) that produce two types of reflections. The two reflections are vertical and horizontal reflections (Berkvens et al., 2014; Bernstein, 1999).

Vertical reflections are interrogations gathered by lecturers on their (past) actions, of curriculum objectives, hardware resources, assessment of learning, physical access, instructor role, hours, face-to-face environment and the content-centered approach (Govender & Khoza, 2017; Khoza, 2017; Mpungose, 2016). Other terms used for the vertical reflections are technical, instrumental, scientific, professional, discipline, reflection-on-action, formal, positivist, content or objective reflections (Maxwell, 2013; Tyler, 2013). All these studies agree that vertical reflections are driven by curriculum objectives as the short-term goals to be achieved by lecturers

Table 2.1 CSW Vertical and Horizontal Reflection Curriculum Concepts

Concepts	Vertical	Horizontal
Goal	Objectives	Outcomes
Content	Literature	Methodology
Community	Physical access	Financial access
Teacher role	Lecturer	Facilitator
Time	Hours	Years
Environment	Face-to-face	Distance
Activity	Content-centered	Societal-centered
Resources	Hardware resources	Software resources
Assessment	Assessment of learning	Assessment as learning

through instructing students to master the content taken from prescribed literature. In vertical reflection, recorded facts, school knowledge and international standards are used in making decisions. Students' performance is measured against international content standards. While vertical reflection may assess what students have learned, it mostly concentrates on what students should have achieved or learned. In other words, it looks for what is still cognitively missing, because students are expected to learn from the lowest content to the highest content of the profession (Budden, 2017; Khoza, 2018). Hardware resources are important because they operate in a linear way that instructs students to follow a plan. For example, resources such as computers require students first to switch them on, login using usernames and passwords and undertake other processes before they access Moodle. Students are defined as those who can have physical access to institutions in order to attend face-to-face classes, answering the "what?" question of teaching and learning (Budden, 2017; Khoza, 2017; Nkohla, 2017). This suggests that students are given adequate professional knowledge as sources of power and to advance their professions. As a result, students learn to plan for their actions in which every hour counts, unlike in horizontal reflection, in which students learn to act from their experiences before they plan.

Horizontal reflections are generated by lecturers in their (present) practices of facilitating students to achieve outcomes per various content (methodologies) sources, assessment as learning, distance learning, and software resources. Students are at different year levels; they are societal-centered, having financial access and lecturers have facilitating roles (Christensen et al., 2001; Hoadley & Jansen, 2014). Other terms used for horizontal reflections are practical, collaborative, reflection-in-action, societal, social, integrated, competence-based, communicative and interpretive reflections (Budden, 2017; Khoza, 2017; Van Manen, 1977). Lecturers and students strive to answer the "how?" question of teaching and learning to achieve the outcomes. Horizontal reflections are driven by achievements of outcomes as students' goals. Content is generated by means of different methodologies/activities from various sources (Hoadley & Jansen, 2014). As a result, assessment is mostly about what is present or what the students have achieved, not what the students should have achieved based on international standards, because prescribed content is very limiting (Cavus, Uzunboylu, & Ibrahim, 2007). Activities involved in the horizontal process are based on problems that affect differing societies of the students. Financial status of students is not a problem because their societies usually take responsibility for student fees. In other words, students develop skills required by their societies. Distance education seems to be important in the horizontal reflections because most students study part time while they are working, and use a variety of digital software resources

(Gay & Kirkland, 2003; Khoza, 2017). Because of the contestation between the two reflections, the findings of this study suggest a new type of reflection that combines these two based on the CSW.

Purpose, Objective and Research Questions

The purpose and objective of the chapter is to explore and understand the lecturers' reflections on the use of CSW concepts at a South African university where they taught and supervised Master of Education (MEd) students in Curriculum Development. The chapter intends to answer the following research questions:

- What are the lecturers' reflections on the use of the CSW concepts in teaching and supervision of Curriculum Development students at a South African university?
- Why do lecturers have particular reflections?

Research Design and Methodology

This case study applied a pragmatic paradigm (Hakim, 2000; Ramrathan, 2017) on 10 lecturers who were involved in teaching and supervision of MEd students within the Curriculum Development department at a South African university. The empirical data on which this chapter is based were generated in 2017 by means of reflective journals and semi-structured interviews. Purposive and convenience samplings (Nieuwenhuis, 2016) were used to choose the most accessible lecturers or supervisors who taught and supervised MEd students. Although the pragmatic case study supports the horizontal reflections more than vertical reflections, re-contextualizing it within diagonal reflection, the case study equally supports both the horizontal and vertical reflections (Budden, 2017; Esau, 2017).

The pragmatic paradigm combines both the qualitative and quantitative methodological paradigms. The application of the pragmatic paradigm, purposive with convenience sampling and data production/gathering methods/instruments, helped me generate rich data about the participants' subjective (Creswell, 2014) reflections through the CSW concepts on Moodle in teaching and supervision. The process helped me to produce an "in-depth understanding that results in a new learning about real-world behaviour and its meaning" (Nieuwenhuis, 2016, p. 5).

The lecturers were invited through electronic mail (email) to participate in the study. They were given consent forms that explained the nature of the study and their rights in terms of confidentiality, anonymity, privacy and withdrawal was there were a need, benefits and ethical principles. Permission was received from gatekeepers, and an ethical clearance letter was obtained from the institution involved.

Reflective journals and semi-structured interviews were conducted twice, in order to triangulate data and enhance the process of trustworthiness. Other principles of trustworthiness which were addressed by this process were credibility (audit trail), dependability (direct quotations from the participants), confirmability (all participants were doing the same job as mine) and transferability (by providing sufficient details of the context), as recommended by Guba and Lincoln (2005) for qualitative studies. Reflective journals were useful because participants completed them in their own time in my absence without any pressure from me, as recommended by other studies (Nieuwenhuis, 2016; Ramrathan, 2017). Interviews were conceptualized as having a clear structure as well as a flexible guide which allowed the participants to share their experiences in their own words (Cohen, Manion, & Morrison, 2011). The strength of the reflective journals was that it gave the participants the opportunity of interrogating their experiences and actions in order to learn from their practices, as recommended by Ramrathan (2017) and Esau (2017).

In this chapter, guided analysis of reflections through CSW utilization was applied for data analysis, in order to generate the new curriculum through horizontal and vertical reflections. Qualitative and quantitative data produced categories (reflection concepts) and themes used for the findings. Guided analysis was useful in this study because it combines inductive and deductive approaches into one strong unit (Samuel, 2009). However, in this chapter, I only report on the qualitative data because I needed the in-depth analyses of the reflections.

Findings and Discussion

The findings are framed by the themes emerging from diagonal/personal reflections. Each of the findings presented under the themes was in written form through the reflective journals of the participants, and was confirmed/triangulated by means of the interviews.

Theme 1: Vertical Curriculum Reflections

Six participants' reflections (Participants 1, 2, 4, 6, 7 and 10) highly recommended the importance of aims (teaching) or purposes (research) and objectives as the goals for their teaching and supervision. "*I use keywords such as introduce, provide, and others for my teaching aims as well as investigate, explore, examine, determine, and others for purposes of my research supervision . . .*" (Participant 1: five of the six agreed). "*I use keywords like understand, know, appreciate and others for my teaching and research work. . . . Research questions do not drive my research work or supervision more than objectives and purpose . . .*" (Participant 2: five of the six agreed). These findings indicate positive use of both the vertical and diagonal reflections. On the one hand, teaching aims and research purposes are defined as habitual long-term goals that represent teachers' and researchers' personal identities or selves (diagonal reflections) (Budden, 2017; Esau, 2017; Schiro, 2013). On the other hand, teaching and research objectives are defined as the short-term goals to be achieved by teachers and researchers through mastering the teaching and research content (Hyland, Kennedy, & Ryan, 2006).

"*When I use CSW in teaching and research supervision I use Moodle* [Modular Object-Oriented Dynamic Learning Environment] *to upload relevant books and studies with relevant module and research content which include relevant theories . . .*" (Participant 10: five of the six agreed). This account suggests that the content concept was used for literature review and research frameworks (theories). Literature review is generated from the research phenomenon in order to address professional needs (vertical), while frameworks are generated from research context to address personal needs (diagonal) (Fomunyam, 2016; Khoza, 2017; Pather, 2017).

"*The strength of CSW concepts in teaching and supervision is the use of my advanced laptops and tablets as well as the application of CHAT, TPACK and other theories . . .*" (Participant 4, the other five agreed). This account indicates the utilization of the hardware (vertical) and ideological-ware resources (diagonal) (Amory, 2012; Govender & Khoza, 2017; Khoza, 2017).

"*. . . I define my students based on their physical and cultural abilities because what make me to be successful in my teaching and supervision . . .*" (Participant 6: the other five agreed). Students' physical abilities represent their profession (vertical) and the culture of students represent their personal identities (Budden, 2017; Nkohla, 2017; Pather, 2017).

"*. . . I use CSW to create teaching and supervision environments that resemble face-to-face and blended learning in order to use what is familiar to students and make each hour and day count . . . activities are always both content and teacher/student centered*" (Participant 2, the other five agreed). A face-to-face environment with content-centered learning monitored over hours is useful if the aims or purposes of teaching or supervision are to advance students' professions; while blended learning with teacher/student-centered learning monitored over days addresses the personal needs (diagonal) (Esau, 2017; Ndlovu, 2017; Nkohla, 2017).

"*. . . I assume my role as a researcher and instructor where I use formative and summative assessments to complement each other . . .*" (Participant 1: the other five agreed). Teaching and supervision as a researcher using formative assessment addresses the needs of individuals while the role of an instructor using formative assessment addresses the needs of one's profession (Hyland et al., 2006; Ndlovu, 2017).

Therefore, the findings for this theme are that, while six of the ten participants reflected positively in both vertical and diagonal reflections of CSW utilization, they reflected negatively in horizontal reflections.

Theme 2: Horizontal Curriculum Reflections

Four participants' reflections (Participants 3, 5, 8 & 9) recommended the importance of outcomes (learning) or research questions (research) and aims (teaching) or purposes (research) as the goals for their teaching and supervision. "... *outcome by its nature is for group of people and it is not for teaching ... as such I use software that help students to achieve outcomes with other students and problem-based activities. ... I always facilitate this process using formative and peer assessments to develop them to become researchers themselves so that by the end of every day or week they achieve different outcomes or answer research questions based on the aims of the module or research projects ... research questions support the purposes of the studies ...*" (Participant 8; the other three participants agreed).

The above accounts suggest that the four participants' reflections were positive on both the horizontal and diagonal reflections but negative on the vertical reflections. Teaching and supervision software, problem-based activities, peer assessment, learning outcomes, research questions, facilitating role and online teaching/supervision are all characteristics of horizontal reflections (Esau, 2017; Khoza, 2017; Ndlovu, 2017). Other concepts such as aims, formative assessment and other of these accounts are repeated in Theme Two to represent the diagonal reflections (Budden, 2017; Hyland et al., 2006; Nkohla, 2017).

In terms of content, "... *I use curriculum concepts to demonstrate and discuss different research methodologies and methods with relevant theoretical frameworks where students are defined in terms of financial access of their community support and cultural access ...*" (Participants 8 and 9 agreed). Participants 3 and 5 indicated that they do not include "*content because students should use their experience based on their cultures through activities ...*" The methodology section of research represents the horizontal reflections, and the framework represents diagonal reflections (Esau, 2017; Fomunyam, 2016; Hamilton & Cobert-Whittier, 2013).

Conclusion and Educational Implications

When the participants had responses of the vertical or horizontal reflections, the concepts of the diagonal reflection (Figure 2.1) were always there

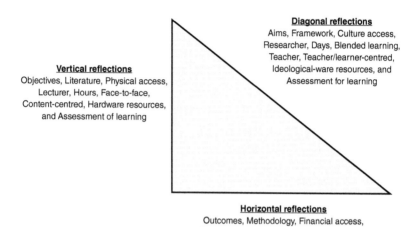

Vertical reflections
Objectives, Literature, Physical access,
Lecturer, Hours, Face-to-face,
Content-centred, Hardware resources,
and Assessment of learning

Diagonal reflections
Aims, Framework, Culture access,
Researcher, Days, Blended learning,
Teacher, Teacher/learner-centred,
Ideological-ware resources, and
Assessment for learning

Horizontal reflections
Outcomes, Methodology, Financial access,
Facilitator, Years, Distance, Societal-centred,
Sofftware resources, and Assessment as learning

Figure 2.1 Curricular Spider Web Reflections

as common factors of the concepts of vertical and horizontal reflections (Figure 2.2). The concepts acted as though they were representing the souls of the participants, as these concepts were reflected through the participants' habitual actions. Habitual actions are what the lecturers do well, whether unconsciously, subconsciously or consciously (Czerniewicz & Brown, 2014). The habitual actions are generated from societal or discipline/professional practices to produce habits or habitual actions that produce lecturers' identities (Khoza, 2018; Pather, 2017). The main aim is to answer the "why?" question of teaching and learning. As a result, habitual actions lead to diagonal reflections, which draw from vertical and horizontal reflections. This suggests that when the vertical reflection produces the performance curriculum (discipline/professional facts) and the horizontal reflection produces the competence-based curriculum (societal opinions) (Hoadley & Jansen, 2014; Reddy & le Grange, 2017), the diagonal reflection may produce a "common factor curriculum" (personal habits). A common factor curriculum should be able to help both lecturers and students to negotiate their ways of combining strengths through the competence-based and the performance-based curriculum. In other words, the common factor curriculum should start with the lecturers' identification and understanding of their own strengths. When lecturers understand their strengths and identities, these assist in controlling performance curriculum (market or discipline driven) and competence-based curriculum (societal or social driven) (Adler, 1991; le Grange, 2016). By having control over curriculum, lecturers are able to decide how much of performance curriculum and/or how much of competence-based curriculum they need in their teaching and supervision to support their students (Budden, 2017; Fomunyam, 2016).

This chapter therefore recommends the understanding of all the "common factor curriculum" propositions through diagonal reflections before curriculum design and development. The concepts are aims/purposes, framework, cultural access, researcher, days, blended learning, teacher/learner-centered, ideological-ware resources (theories), assessment for learning, as shown in Figure 2.2. Table 2.2 below compares the common factor curriculum concepts when they are used in teaching and research.

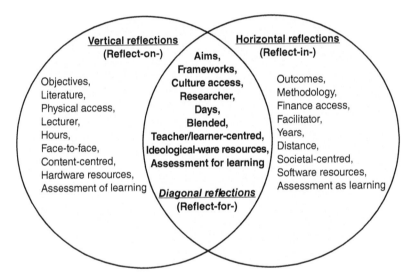

Figure 2.2 Diagonal as a Common Factor

Table 2.2 Common Factor Curriculum Propositions in Teaching and Research

Concept	Teaching	Research
Reason	Pragmatic	Personal
Goal	Aim	Purpose
Community	Student culture	Participant/respondent culture
Content	Teaching philosophy	Paradigm/theoretical framework
Assessment	Assessment for learning	Data collection methods
Lecturer Role	Researcher	Researcher
Time	Each day frame	Each day frame
Environment	Blended learning	Blended learning
Activity	Lecturer-centered	Researcher-centered
Resource	Lecturers' habitual actions	Researchers' habitual actions

References

Adler, A. (1991). The reflective of teacher and the curriculum of teacher education. *Journal of Education for Teaching, 17*(2), 139–150.

Amory, A. (2012). Tool-mediated authentic learning in an educational technology course: A designed-based innovation. *Interactive Learning Environments* (ahead-of-print), 1–17.

Badat, S. (2010). *The challenges of transformation in higher education and training institutions in South Africa.* Johannesburg: Development Bank of Southern AfricaIlahan, R.M.

Berkvens, J., van den Akker, J., & Brugman, M. (2014). *Addressing the quality challenge: Reflections on the post-2015 UNESCO education agenda.* Enschede: Netherlands National Commission for UNESCO.

Bernstein, B. (1999). Vertical and horizontal discourse: An essay. *British Journal of Sociology of Education, 20*(2), 157–173.

Budden, R. (2017). *Exploration of factors that inform curriculum studies students to use e-resources in conducting masters of education dissertations at a South African university.* (Doctor of Philosophy Full research), University of KwaZulu-Natal, Durban. (1).

Cavus, N., Uzunboylu, H., & Ibrahim, D. (2007). Assessing the success rate of students using a learning management system together with a collaborative tool in web-based teaching of programming languages. *Journal of educational computing research, 36*(3), 301–321.

Christensen, L. M., Wilson, E. K., Anders, S. K., Dennis, M. B., Kirkland, L., Beacham, M., & Warren, E. P. (2001). Teachers' reflections on their practice of social studies. *The Social Studies, 92*(5), 205–208.

Cohen, L., Manion, L., & Morrison, K. (2011). *Research methods in education* (7th ed.). New York: Routledge.

Creswell, J. W. (2014). *Qualitative inquiry and research design: Choosing among five approaches* (3rd ed.). Thousand Oaks, CA: Sage Publications, Inc.

Czerniewicz, L., & Brown, C. (2014). The habitus and technological practices of rural students: A case study. *South African Journal of Education, 34*(1), 1–14.

Dewey, J. (1933). *How we think: A restatement of reflective thinking to the educative process.* Boston, MA: Heath.

Esau, O. (2017). Emancipatory action research. In L. Ramrathan, L. Le Grange, & P. Higgs (Eds.), *Education studies: For initial teacher development* (pp. 444–455). Cape Town: Juta & Company (Pty) LTD.

Fomunyam, K. G. (2016). *Content and ideology in literature modules taught in a Cameroonian university* (Doctor of Philosophy Full thesis), University of KwaZulu-Natal, Durban. (1).

Gay, G., & Kirkland, K. (2003). Developing cultural critical consciousness and self-reflection in preservice teacher education. *Theory into Practice, 42*(3), 181–187.

Govender, N., & Khoza, S. B. (2017). Technology in education for teachers. In L. Ramrathan, L. Le Grange, & P. Higgs (Eds.), *Education studies for initial teacher development* (pp. 66–79). Cape Town: Juta & Company (Pty) LTD.

Guba, E. G., & Lincoln, Y. S. (2005). Paradigmatic controversies, contradictions, and emerging confluences. In N. K. Denzin & Y. S. Lincoln (Eds.), *Handbook of qualitative research* (3rd ed., pp. 191–216). London: Sage Publications, Inc.

Hakim, C. (2000). *Research design: Successful designs for social and economic research.* New York: Routledge.

Hamilton, L., & Cobert-Whittier, C. (2013). *Using case study in education research.* London: Sage Publications, Inc.

Hoadley, U., & Jansen, J. (2014). *Curriculum: Organizing knowledge for the classroom* (3rd ed.). Cape Town: Oxford University Press Southern Africa.

Hyland, A., Kennedy, D., & Ryan, N. (2006). *Writing and using learning outcomes: A practical guide.* Bologna: European Higher Education Area (EHEA).

Khoza, S. B. (2017, June 1–2). *Is this Moodle for personal, societal and/or professional space/s when students reflect?* Paper presented at the 12th International Conference on E-Learning (ICEL), The Central University of Florida, Orlando.

Khoza, S. B. (2018). Can teachers' reflections on digital and curriculum resources generate lessons? *Africa Education Review, 1,* 1–16. doi:10.1080/18146627.201 7.1305869

Khoza, S. B., & Manik, S. (2015). The recognition of "Digital Technology Refugees" amongst post graduate students in a higher education institution. *Alternation, 17,* 190–208.

le Grange, L. (2016). Decolonising the university curriculum. *South African Journal of Higher Education, 30*(2), 1–12.

Maxwell, T. W. (2013). A model for reflection to be used in authentic assessment in teacher education. *Journal of the International Society for Teacher Education, 17*(1), 8–17.

Mpungose, C. B. (2016). *Teachers' reflections of the teaching of grade 12 physical sciences CAPS in rural schools at Ceza circuit* (Master of Education), University of KwaZulu-Natal, Durban.

Ndlovu, B. N. (2017). *Exploring teachers' understanding of pedagogic practices in teaching mathematical concepts in grade 1: A case study in South African primary schools* (Doctor of Philosophy Full thesis), University of KwaZulu-Natal, Durban. (1).

Nieuwenhuis, J. (2016). Qualitative research designs and data-gathering techniques. In K. Maree (Ed.), *First steps in research* (3rd ed., pp. 72–100). Pretoria: Van Schaik.

Nkohla, M. B. (2017). *Educators' reflections on their practices of agricultural sciences curriculum and assessment policy statement* (Master of Education), University of KwaZulu-Natal, Durban.

Pather, R. (2017). *Library spaces in higher education: Exploring academics' understanding.* (Doctor of Philosophy Full thesis), University of KwaZulu-Natal, Durban. (1).

Pinar, W. F. (2012). *What is curriculum theory?* New York, NY: Routledge.

Prensky, M. (2001). Digital natives, digital immigrants part 1. *On the Horizon, 9*(5), 1–6.

Ramrathan, L. (2017). Educational research: Key concepts. In L. Ramrathan, L. Le Grange, & P. Higgs (Eds.), *Education studies: For initial teacher development* (pp. 403–418). Cape Town: Juta & Company (Pty) LTD.

Reddy, C., & le Grange, L. (2017). Assessment and curriculum. In L. Ramrathan, L. Le Grange, & P. Higgs (Eds.), *Education studies: For initial teacher development* (pp. 159–173). Cape Town: Juta & Company (Pty) LTD.

Rushkof, D. (2006). *Screenagers: Lessons in Chaos from digital kids.* Hampton: Incorporated Hampton Press.

Samuel, M. A. (2009). *On becoming a teacher: Life history research and the force-field model of teacher development.* In R. Dhunpath & M. A. Samuel (Eds.), *Life history research-epistemology, methodology and representation.* Rotterdam: Sense Publishers.

Schiro, M. S. (2013). *Curriculum theory: Conflicting visions and enduring concerns* (2nd ed.). Thousand Oaks, CA: Sage Publications, Inc.

Schön, D. A. (1983). *The reflective practitioner.* New York, NY: Basic Books.

Tyler, R. W. (2013). *Basic principles of curriculum and instruction.* Chicago, IL: University of Chicago Press.

Van den Akker, J. (2003). *Curriculum perspectives: An introduction.* Enschede: Netherlands Institute for Curriculum Development.

Van Manen, M. (1977). Linking ways of knowing with ways of being practical. *Curriculum Inquiry, 6,* 205–212.

3 Language and Academic Literacies Development at the University of Johannesburg

Guy R. Mihindou

Introduction

The current language and academic literacies strategy at the University of Johannesburg (UJ) seems not only fragmented in its approaches but also overwhelming vis-à-vis the student's level of competence and their ability to overcome their own deficit. This chapter will present the status quo of language and academic literacies at UJ and will contextualize possible pragmatic academic and language literacies solutions. Any attempt at detailing strategies aimed at addressing literacies issues at the University is overwhelming. The challenge is not so much about jotting down a few ideas that may be implemented; it is rather about the choice of an appropriate framework, and the implication thereof, as many attempts have been made before. The objective is to determine what already has been achieved, before benchmarking the current usage of literacies against national trends. Consequently, some internal literatures helped to map the way, and staffs were interviewed to establish the appropriateness of the institution's discourse on language and academic literacies.

Moreover, the multifaceted aspects of language issues as experienced in South African universities justify a need to contextualize the problem of literacies at UJ. It is an African University; as such, any proposed solutions need guidance by two facts: the majority of the student population experiences and the problem of literacies at higher education (HE) institutions in South Africa. This may be in contrast to the United States and Europe whose literature is abundant and influences significantly the current literacies' discourse; and the problem of literacies experienced at UJ is national, historical and complex. As such, no quick fix is to be expected and a solution for such complexity should be driven by collaborative efforts.

The nomenclature from De Kadt's (2012) proposition, the benchmarked reading report compiled by Damons and Kane (2011) and the NBT results of 2012 are at the center of this chapter. Vongo's (2005) thesis based on a case study exploring the goals of a business communication course at the then Technikon Witwatersrand (TWR) is another piece of work that guided internal UJ literatures. An additional document consulted is the National Benchmark Test Project (NBTP) of 2013, whose report gives a criterion-referenced view of the results of candidates who applied at UJ. The significance of this document is measured against the backdrop of the internal data generated by Van Zyl on the profile of UJ students. Van Zyl's data highlights some endogenous and exogenous causes of the literacies problem/ phenomenon.

The intention of writing the present work was also to propose some models that may work well at UJ. Hence the proposition of three models as a basis upon which the language and academic literacies may take shape. Henceforth three main sections: (1) the point of departure; (2) the language literacies discourse at UJ; and (3) the proposed models for language and literacies needed.

1. Point of Departure

The objective of the chapter is to establish a framework of language and literacies at UJ and propose some workable ways of addressing the issue of literacies. The current strategy seems not only fragmented in its approaches but also overwhelming vis-à-vis the student's level of competence and their ability to overcome their own deficit. The response to such a need requires collaboration among all parties involved in HE institutions in order to achieve the academic development of the students.

Gustafsson (2011, p. 1) argues that a genuine literacies approach in HE is already disciplinary by necessity. He adds that even if we do not have an immediate disciplinary context to work in, we still need to work with the students' understanding of the communities they are active with. Shabanza (2014) highlights the role that academic literacies development initiatives have played in both widening students' access to South African HE and contributing towards the improvement of the student's success rate, and proposes two major approaches: writing across the curriculum (WAC) and writing in the discipline (WID).

The term literacy/literacies in its plural or singular form is evocative of the lack of unanimity among scholars about its use. The use of the plural form "academic literacies" has been chosen to indicate a specific epistemological and ideological approach towards academic writing and communication (Lillis & Scott, 2007). The stand plurality of "literacies" refers to the positioning of "academic literacies" as an applied field, which has to not only face research communities, but also the institution in which its users work and seek to influence the approach to literacies issues (Lillis &

Scott, 2007). The pluralized term makes it possible to recognize that to be academically literate is more than being able to produce an academic essay. Thus, "literacy" is best viewed not as *learning programmes* but as activities which everyone engages in, in the course of operating within their life-worlds (Lea & Street, 2011, p. 368). Because of the fluidity of academic literacies in terms of their forms and applicability, the understanding of literacies discourse at a tertiary institution ought to be approached from contextualized perspectives.

2. Language and Literacies Discourse at UJ

Discussions about how best to enhance students' learning experience at UJ in general and vis-à-vis literacy in particular have taken place. The existence of departments and centers such as Applied Communication Skills (ACS), Academic Development Centre (ADC) and the language center whose aim is to deal with issues pertaining to language and literacies denotes the inten-tion of UJ to offer adequate support to students in need. However, despite UJ's constant effort to help students, the observation of academic staff is that the students' literacy competences have not improved to the desired expectation.

Van Zyl (2012) indicates that first generation students (whose relatives never studied at university before) present a serious lack of vibrant liter-acy habits that they should have had from home, and the culture of reading is non-existent, whereas writing is just done when requested by lecturers for assessment purposes. Moreover, these students seem not to be aware of various interventions designed in an attempt to reduce the literacy deficit observed in their NBT results.

Damons and Kane (2011), citing the UJ NBT working group, explain that in order to cope successfully at the tertiary level and be considered proficient, students need to attain an academic literacy score of 65% or above. Selected results of the 2011 NBT reveal that many students admitted to UJ that par-ticular year did not achieve this threshold. Out of 4,408 students involved in a First Year Experience (FYE) survey, only 744, or 16.88%, scored "profi-cient"; 2,706, or 61.39%, scored "intermediate"; and 958, or 21.73%, scored "basic" (Van Zyl, 2011).

It is possible that students in a mass system do not necessarily share the aims and assumptions of disciplinary specialists when they first enter univer-sity (Haggis, 2006). They sometimes question the relevance of the support offered to them, as they regard it as a repetition of high school programmes (Vongo, 2005, p. 1).

The last point above suggests that the question could be twofold: what is the students' role and responsibility concerning taking their studies seriously;

and, to what extent would the university guarantee the efficiency of the intervention and the quality of the content offered to students while ensuring that it does not turn into "spoon-feeding schemes"?

2.1 Unrealistic Expectations

Vongo (2005, p. 2) suggests that the goals of service English courses are not clear enough to students. He asserts that these goals are more implicit than explicit. Consequently, he argues that course design would benefit much if the goals of English service courses are subjected to an inspection. Vongo (2005, p. 2) infers that the three major stakeholders: students, lecturers and heads of schools have different views and, therefore, come to different understandings of the purposes of these goals. It is therefore unsurprising that they have unrealistic expectations.

The trends observed by Vongo (2005, p. 54) at the then TWR, in 2005, are still to a certain degree relevant and vivid at UJ in 2017. Indeed, he points out that 86% of students used and still consider English as their second language (ESL), while 6% used and viewed English as their first language.

2.2 The Impact of Reading

Damons and Kane (2011) highlight the impact of reading on the development of writing skills. They caution that, "the absence of reading has a direct impact on students" writing' (see Horning, 2007: 9). In Horning's view, reported by Damons and Kane (2011), reading forms the basis of academic writing across disciplines. As such, reading and writing ought to be taught side-by-side. Reading often serves as a stimulus for writing projects, and writing can be used to deepen the understanding of what has been read. Furthermore, if students are not exposed to substantial reading in the genres of a particular discipline, they will be unable to produce discipline-specific writing when required to do so.

2.3 Reading and Plagiarism

In addition to the importance of reading, Damons and Kane (2011) corroborate the view expressed by Horning about reading, indicating the relationship between reading and plagiarism. Horning suggests that plagiarism is not a problem of ethics or morality, but rather, a reading problem; it is a "byproduct of students' inability to read" and synthesize what they have read to support an argument in an academically acceptable way (2007, p. 10). Therefore, one of the ways in which lecturers can combat plagiarism is to ensure that students have acquired the requisite reading-related skills (e.g., the ability to paraphrase, summarize, analyze, evaluate and so forth).

2.4 The Status of Reading and Writing at UJ in Contrast with Other Universities

In Table 3.1 below, Damons and Kane (2011, p. 8) present, in a synoptic manner, the status of student reading at UJ and compared with those of other South African universities.

Table 3.1 The Status of Students' Reading at UJ Compared to Some South African Universities

Testing of students	At University of Pretoria (UP), Northwest University (NWU) and Stellenbosch University (SU), all first-year students are required to write the TALL or TAG language proficiency placement test. Students are then placed in appropriate academic literacies courses. University of the Western Cape (UWC) does not require its students to write a test in order to register for the academic literacies modules. At UJ, only first year students write the NBT tests, but these tests are not used for placement.
Reading as part of a module	At UP, EOT 161 is a seven week/one quarter long module worth six credits. Students attend three times a week. The module focuses on reading theory, speed-reading, reading strategies and vocabulary. At NWU, the academic literacies module is a yearlong module focusing not only on reading but also on other academic literacies. At SU, the Language Centre's Unit presents academic literacies modules for Afrikaans and English. This module bears 12 credits and focuses on reading and writing. At UJ, reading is part of both the Mastering of Academic Professional Skills (MAPS) and academic literacies modules offered by the Academic Development Centre. These modules are worth 12 credits.
Where reading is situated	The Unit of Academic Literacy presents at UP, an academic reading module, whereas Read-On is offered by the School of Engineering and Support Services. At NWU, the School of Languages presents the module. At SU, the Unit presents modules for Afrikaans and English Language. At UWC, the module is presented by academic literacy and teaching and learning specialists. At UJ, the Learning Development and Academic Literacies Units of the Academic Development Centre present modules integrating reading. They have also used Read-On to a certain extent. In addition, language specialists from the Academic Literacies Unit of ADC have begun to assist lecturers with the integration of reading skills into course content.

(Continued)

Table 3.1 (Continued)

Electronic reading programmes	NWU, UP and UJ make use of the Read-On programme.
	At the NWU's Potchefstroom campus, there is a reading lab with reading assistants. A full-time staff member monitors student progress and provides support to struggling students. Students are contacted if they miss classes. Students are assisted if they require support. This approach could be considered by UJ.
	Members of staff at NWU have researched and proposed a three-tier system, of which Read-On is one component. However, this approach does not seem to have been implemented.
	At UP, all students are required to take the TALL or TAG for placement purposes. Students in need of reading support are placed in EOT 101, an academic reading course. Students requiring further support are referred to support services that offer Read-On. However, no follow-up on the progress of students enrolled in Read-On is undertaken. The Read-On programme is also offered in the School of Engineering as part of the ENGAGE module. This module is credit bearing and runs throughout the year. The students are allocated one period per week; but they are also required to work an additional two hours per week outside of class. In addition, lecturers present lessons on reading skills and reading strategies. Depending on how UJ structures its reading programme, lessons on different reading skills and strategies could also be valuable for some UJ students.
	At UJ, mainstream students are required to complete the Read-On programme in their own time. The programme has unfortunately been discontinued.

2.5   Coordinated Strategy as a Prerequisite for a Lasting Solution to Students' Unpreparedness

De Kadt's (2012, p. 1) comments on the 2012 UJ NBT test indicate that 85% of students were not proficient enough and could need substantial academic literacies support. Table 3.2 shows students' results in NBT test and the level of support they may require.

De Kadt (2012) affirms that the results of the NBT test corroborate UJ's academic staff's growing concerns about decreasing levels of linguistic ability. This is against the backdrop of the fact that poor language proficiency is recognized nationally and internationally as being the core factor in students' underperformance and failure. She notes that a number of well-considered developmental initiatives are already in place at UJ. However, she stresses that individual initiatives, without broader backing, cannot adequately address this challenge; what is needed is a concerted and well-structured institutional strategy.

Table 3.2 Students' Results in NBT Test and the Level of Support They May Require

Proficient	"Academic progress not likely to be affected"	14.4%
Intermediate	"Academic progress likely to be affected": extended or augmented programmes recommended	57.9%
Basic	"Serious learning challenges identified": extensive and long-term support required, e.g. bridging programme or FET college	27.7%

n = 5734 (NBT results of 2012 De Kadt, 2012)

2.6 Assistance Currently Offered to Students at UJ

2.6.1 Reading Academically

At UJ, reading development is integrated into augmented modules in the faculties and within the academic literacies modules offered to first year extended degree students by the ADC. Various reading skills and competencies of students are developed throughout the year. These include academic reading, reading with understanding, critical reading, construction of argument, reading strategies, annotation of texts, note-making, note-taking, summarizing, paraphrasing and so on.

2.6.2 Academic Writing

The transformative nature of writing centers at UJ helps and facilitates the literacies agenda and pushes to tackle the language problem within its facilities at three levels among its student population: the coercive, voluntary and collaborative methods.

The coercive method is not practical presently due to an absence of a clear language and literacies policy that may guide and guarantee a successful implementation on a day-to-day basis. The voluntary method, which allows students to attend writing center workshops and permit booking for consultations freely, is currently in use at UJ and focuses on two of the three academic literacies matrixes: high order and middle order matters.

The collaborative method, which consists of a stronger engagement between the language specialist and various lecturers in faculties, has generated a new way of thinking in academic literacies matters at UJ. There has been a migration from writing across the curriculum (WAC) to writing in the disciple (WID). It is this last method that is most effective and has positioned the writing center activities at the center of language and academic literacies within the university.

2.6.4 Communication Skills Course

The department of applied communication, within the faculty of humanities, offers the communication skills course, tailored according to the need expressed by stakeholders. The objective of the course is the transitioning of students from high school to university by emphasizing the following:

- Non-verbal communication
- Multicultural communication
- Organizational communication
- Oral presentations skills
- Basic communication theory

2.6.5 UJ English Language Programme (UJELP)

The UJELP is designed to address the language issues confronted by international students at the university, usually from non-English-speaking countries. The rationale underpinning the establishment of UJELP is the provision of a clear strategy to improve its international profile and participation, driven mainly by the division for Internationalization and the Faculties.

3. The Proposed Models

The work of Lea and Street (1998) describe three models: 1) the study skills model; 2) the academic socialization model; and 3) the academic literacies model. These models I suggest should frame the LSS-offered to guide, assist and prepare students for the challenges of academic life and beyond; UJELP offered to facilitate international students' reading, writing, speaking and listening skills for both communicative and academic purposes; and the Undergraduate Language and Literacies course (ULLC) modules.

The study skills model focuses on the surface features of writing and postulates that the learners' transfer of writing skills and literacy from one context to the other occurs without any problem. *The academic socialization model* aims to acculturate students into the disciplinary discourses and genres, which are considered as stable enough. They are based on the presumption that students will be able to reproduce these discourses and genres once they have understood and practiced the applicable rules.

The academic literacies model revolves around the concepts of power and authority, meaning making and identity. It foregrounds institutional prescriptions of what can be considered as knowledge in specific academic contexts, and the students' attitudes towards these prescriptions. The academic literacies model differs from the academic socialization model in that it views the process of acquisition of relevant and effective literacies as more complex, dynamic, nuanced, situated and embedded in epistemological issues and social processes, including social identities, power relations and institutional practices. Lea and Street's work shape/should shape academic literacies practice and research at UJ.

Conclusion

Academic literacies research has developed over the past 20 years as a significant field of study that draws on a number of disciplinary fields and subfields including applied linguistics, sociolinguistics, anthropology, sociocultural theories of learning, new literacy studies and discourse studies. In spite of the fluidity and confusion surrounding the use of the term "academic literacies" (Lillis & Scott, 2007), this text used the plural form of this terms for the strategic reasons explained from the onset.

The importance of reading cannot be underestimated, as it constitutes the other side of the same coin with writing, being on the one side albeit in the discipline (WID) or across the curriculum (WAC), as explained earlier. A benchmarking exercise to look into the academic literacies development projects of other institutions of higher learning was necessary to position UJ's own practices vis-à-vis reading and writing, as these urgently require contextualized strategies. The proposed strategies have been exemplified in the form of models; each represents a unique perspective of what is already happening at UJ or will soon take place.

References

Damons, V., & Kane, S. (2011, October). *Reading benchmarking report*. Academic Development Centre, UJ.

Dekadt, E. (2012.) *UJ strategy on English language development at undergraduate level*. Unpublished.

Gustafsson, M. (2011). Academic literacies approaches for facilitating language for specific purposes *Ibérica, 22*, 101–122, ISSN 1139–7241

Haggis, T. (2006, October). Pedagogies for diversity: Retaining critical challenge amidst fears of "dumbing down". *Studies in Higher Education, 31*(5), 521–535.

Horning, A. S. (2007). *Reading across the Curriculum as the key to student success*. Retrieved from https://wac.colostate.edu/atd/articles/horning2007.cfm

Hyland, K. (2002). Genre: Language, context, and literacy. *Annual Review of Applied Linguistics, 22*, 113–135. Retrieved September 18, 2014, from http://love wonder.sg1006.myweb.hinet.net/Integrated%20Course/GENRE--LANGUAGE, %20CONTEXT,%20AND%20LITERACY.pdf

Lea, M. & Street, B. (1998). The "Academic Literacies" model: Theory and Application. Retrieved from https://www.researchgate.net/publication/47343136_The_ Academic_Literacies_Model_Theory_and_Applications

Lea, M., & Street, B. (2011). *The "Academic Literacies" model: Theory and applications*. Retrieved September 17, 2014, from www.jstor.org/discover/10.2307/40071 622?uid=2129&uid=2&uid=70&uid=4&sid=21104179286781

Lillis, T., & Scott, M. (2007). Defining academic literacies research: Issues of epistemology, ideology and strategy. *Journal of Applied Linguistics, 4*(1), 5–32.

Shabanza, K. J. (2014). *Integration of academic literacies into the disciplines: An overview*. Unpublished discussion document.

Van Zyl, A. (2011). *Survey results on the student profile questionnaire*. University of Johannesburg.

Van Zyl, A. (2012). *Survey results on the student profile questionnaire*. University of Johannesburg.

Vongo, M. R. (2005). *A case study of the goals of the business communication course at Technikon* (Med thesis), Rhodes University, Unpublished.

Theme 2

Fair Access

What strategies are being utilized or could be utilized in institutions of higher learning in South Africa to guarantee fair access to qualified individuals in management, staffing and student recruitment from all cultural backgrounds?

4 (UN)trapped? Transformative Voices of Four Black Female "Novice" Academics in a South African Higher Education Institution

Ncamisile P. Mthiyane, Zanele Heavy-Girl Dube-Xaba, Maserole Christina Kgari-Masondo, and Fumane P. Khanare

Introduction

While efforts to transform higher education (HE) have gained pace in South Africa in the past two decades, more platforms need to be created to attract previously excluded groups, particularly Black women, from a range of social contexts. This chapter presents a descriptive analysis of the lived experiences and career development of four Black female "novice" academics (BFNA) in a selected South African higher education institution (HEI). It draws on critical consciousness theory (CCT) and an asset-based framework to highlight their voices as critical assets in strengthening transformation of HE.

A "novice" is a person who is new to and inexperienced in a job or situation (Quin, 2012; McArthur-Rouse, 2008). Generally "novice" researchers/academics experience a number of challenges, including their roles and responsibilities which are teaching, research and community engagement (Chester & Espelin, 2003; Remmik, Karm, Haamer, & Lepp, 2011; Quin, 2012). While a "novice" academic might demonstrate sound content and pedagogical knowledge, they are still regarded as "novices" because they lack strength in journal publications and supervision. In the institution where this study was conducted, academics at lecturer level are regarded as "novices" whether or not they have published in scientific journals or supervised and graduated Masters students. Only once one becomes a senior lecturer does one qualify as a seasoned academic and researcher.

Current developments in educational transformation in South Africa revolve around transformation *by* the people and *with* the people. In our view, it is impossible to promote the transformation of HE without meaningfully involving those in HEIs. The current institutional landscape offers wide-ranging platforms to advance transformation (Higgs, 2016). Section 1.12 of the *White Paper 3: A Programme for the Transformation of Higher Education* (Department of Education, 1997) notes that:

> . . . economic and technological changes create an agenda for the role of higher education in reconstruction and development. This includes: Human resource development: the mobilisation of human talent and potential through lifelong learning to contribute to the social, economic, cultural and intellectual life of a rapidly changing society.

It adds that Black academics, including those regarded as "novice," are key participants in such an agenda (DoE, 1997). The term Black includes South Africans classified as Africans, Indians and Coloreds that suffered discrimination in the apartheid past (Alexander, 2006).

Current Status of Transformation in Higher Education

The literature shows that transformation of South African HE is slow and that discrimination and inequalities based on a range of characteristics shaped, and continue to shape, this sector (Badat, 2010; Boughey, 2007). The 1996 South African Constitution and the Higher Education Act and White Paper of 1997 directed HEIs on how to achieve fundamental transformation. For example, the *Reflections on Higher Education Transformation Discussion Paper* (2015) calls for the active removal of any institutional, social, material and intellectual barriers to ensure a more equal, inclusive and socially just HE system. The Constitution requires that all South African institutions affirm the values and freedoms set out in the Bill of Rights (Republic of South Africa, 1996). However, the literature notes that the HE system still has a long way to go in terms of contributing to social justice, development and democratic citizenship (Badat, 2010; Chimanikire, Mutandwa, Gadzirayi, Muzondo, & Mutandwa, 2007).

In many respects, universities' structures, cultures and practices continue to operate as powerful mechanisms of social exclusion and injustice. Badat (2010) notes that HEIs have not been effective in attracting and retaining staff from previously disadvantaged groups, especially Black women academics. The Higher Education Act (1997) aimed to create a single co-ordinated HE system (Badat, 2010; DoE, 1997). It identifies the principles and values that should be promoted including equity, redress and mobilizing human talent and potential. A democratic environment that accommodates the needs of academic staff from previously disadvantaged backgrounds is essential (Boughey, 2007). However, the racial and gendered inequities in the composition of university staff indicate that structural obstacles persist (Naicker, 2013; DoE, 2008). This calls for cohesion and wide-ranging transformation

(Dominguez-Whitehead & Moosa, 2014). Kadi-Hanifi's (2013) study of four Black lecturers concluded that the core requirement for success within and across HE is collegial supportive networks. It is also essential to identify and understand covert and systemic inequalities. The participants in Bartman's (2015) study on Black women's multiple marginalization in HEIs identified historically Black sororities as positive support structures.

Theoretical Framework

Hearing multiple voices on how transformation is conceptualized is rooted in the African adage, *lets'oele le beta poho* (a crowd defeats a bull). In terms of CCT (Freire, 1973) and the asset-based approach (ABA) (Kretzmann & McKnight, 1993), BFNA are not constructed as a burden and deficit in the transformation process. "The unifying thread of his [Freire's] work is critical consciousness as a motor of cultural emancipation" (Goulet, 1974, p. vii). Therefore, active participation in the critique of knowledge production is required to transform South African HE (Swanagan, 2014). Kretzmann and McKnight (1993) advocate for the development and empowerment of communities from the inside out (ibid). Ebersöhn and Eloff (2006) note that ABA recognizes that even among marginalized people there exists a pool of assets, skills and resources that can be used to create a more effective community.

Research Methodology

We use a transformative paradigm (Creswell, 2014) that foregrounds "marginalized" voices and seeks to make them heard as agents to improve their own lives and those of others. This is similar to the Sesotho and iSiZulu proverbs: *"ngoana sa lleng o shoela tharing"* and *"ingane engakhali ifela embelekweni"* (literally, a child who does not cry will die on the mother's back). The transformative paradigm aims to create a sense of consciousness where we begin to question, reflect and understand our positions in an HEI and how such knowledge could enable agency for transformation (Mitchell, 2011; Ukpokudu, 2010). We adopt a narrative inquiry to provide insights into our experiences as members of a social, work-based initiative for transformation in HE. According to Webster and Mertova (2007) and Bruner (2004), narrative researchers foreground the participant's story, explore the meaning of individual experiences and shape new theoretical understanding of people's experiences. We draw on qualitative data from two unconventional data generation methods (Maree, 2013), namely, safe space technologies including informal discussion, and free writing reflections, supported by discussions from formal meetings to facilitate data triangulation.

Zihlobo Zesafe Space Network

Zihlobo is a Zulu word meaning "my relatives." Zihlobo Zesafe Space Net-work (Zihlobo) is a social network group that was initiated in 2016 during "corridor talk," conversations and exchange of e-mails. There are currently seven members, four women and three men. We meet once a week to share our content knowledge and pedagogical skills, research and home-related challenges and celebrate our successes. In this chapter, we reflect on the experiences of the four BFNA members that were purposively selected. They satisfied the following criteria: they are Black female academics in the early years of supervising MEd and PhD students; serve as co-ordinators of disciplines/modules and completed their PhDs between 2008 and 2016 in different fields and universities. They also serve on School committees. While new or "novice" to the academy, they have a wealth of experience in their respective fields and play leadership roles in their communities.

All ethical protocols set by the University Research Office and Research Ethics Committee were observed. Pseudonyms are used to ensure confiden-tiality and anonymity (Cohen, Manion, & Morrison, 2011). Trustworthiness was ensured by triangulating written narratives, reflections and discussions/dialogues. A brief profile of each BFNA is provided below.

Fumza

Fumza is a full-time lecturer with two years' experience as a discipline head in Educational Psychology, within the School of Education and teaches in its postgraduate (PG) programmes. She served as an academic qualification coordinator for the PG certificate in education for two years and academic coordinator for BEd Honours; and was a committee member in the Initial Teacher Education Programme. She taught in secondary schools before join-ing the university as a post-graduate student and was subsequently appointed as a lecturer. While doing her Honours, Masters and PhD, she was a research assistant on one of her supervisors' research projects.

Yellow-Bone

Yellow-bone is a full-time undergraduate and PG lecturer. She has served as the head of Life Orientation Discipline within the School of Education; a member of the School Board, Examinations Board and other commit-tees. She previously worked as a junior and senior primary teacher, head of department (HoD), deputy principal and acting principal, and as a part-time lecturer in HE.

Za

Za is a full-time lecturer in Tourism Education and is serving her fifth year as the head of discipline. She teaches in the undergraduate and PG programmes and serves on School committees. Before joining the university, Za worked at a high school and served as an educator, HOD, deputy principal, Senior Education Specialist and Deputy Chief Education Specialist. She always looked forward to teaching at the university and applied for positions at different institutions.

Kgotsi

Kgotsi is a full-time lecturer in History, Geography and Social Science in the School of Education. She teaches undergraduate and PG students and is an ordained Pastor, Apostle and Bishop. She obtained her MA at the University of Cape Town (UCT) and PhD from Stellenbosch University and was awarded a scholarship from the Mellon Foundation. While working as a teacher, she tutored at UCT and was later employed at an HEI as a postdoctoral fellow and lecturer.

Data Generation: Zihlobo's Dialogues

The transformative paradigm liberates us from conventional prescriptive data generation methods and seeks to decolonize traditional research methods (Creswell, 2014). Zihlobo is a democratic space that enables information sharing and debate using dialogue, jokes, stories and reflection (MacDonald, 2012).

The data was generated through free writing reflections (Mitchell, 2011) and whole group discussions (Maree, 2013; Flick, 2014). After an initial meeting with Zihlobo members to explain the nature of the study and obtain a general overview of their experiences, the second meeting involved free writing reflections. This was preceded by a discussion on the prompts outlined by Mitchell (2011) that guided the reflections. Following critical debate, the following three questions emerged to guide the written reflections:

- How did you feel on getting a job in a HEI?
- What are the experiences, successes/challenges of teaching in a HEI?
- How do you think you can transform yourself/space within the HEI?

In the third stage, data was generated using whole group discussion, with each member presenting her reflections to the group and questions for clarity. Data were recorded, transcribed and analyzed thematically (Braun & Clarke, 2006).

Themes were independently developed by each of the four researchers and then synthesized through discussion, theoretical reflection, searching for counter-examples and re-writing. In the final stage of analysis, similarities were identified among the participants' trajectories.

Amaphupho (Dreams)

The four BFNA seem to have been socialized into the journey of transformation before teaching in the HEI. Kgotsi sought to overcome her orphanhood and become an agent of change (Ukpokudu, 2010):

> It took my painful background as an orphan not to be trapped in a state of self-pity and I managed to study and qualify for all my degrees to PhD.

Fumza recalled that her grandmother, who had no formal education, encouraged her to excel. Her "induction" into learning promoted her transformation as well as that of her family and community:

> . . . to have a PhD, being a Black female in my family and village was a dream come true . . . indeed my achievements were my family's and community's achievements.

Za and Yellow-bone's entry into HE was not as closely connected to their families and they primarily reflected on their previous work experiences. Yellow-bone lectured part-time at an HEI and Za knew "the ropes" of searching for a job in HEIs. The latter recalled:

> At first, I lacked technology skills and was unsuccessful but learnt a lot from that experience. As a Black female . . . from a historically marginalised group that was under-represented in academia, I was very eager to join the HEI. . . . In the following year the same position was advertised and I was successful.

Yellow-bone wanted a more challenging job:

> . . . I was employed as a Tutor while in my final year of Master's degree and years later teaching in the National Professional Diploma in Education and Advanced Certificate in Education programmes. I became bored after some time in schools.

As an experienced teacher and HOD, she mentored a number of newly qualified teachers and identified gaps between pre-service and in-service teachers.

She felt that in an HEI, she could assist student teachers with pedagogical methods.

Thus, transformation is embedded in these academics' lives. Attributes such as caring for their family, teachers, learners, and parents and job satisfaction motivated them to enter HEIs.

Transformative Voices Within the Academe: Enablers and Constraints

The enablers and constraints of transformation within the academe was another overarching theme.

Peer-Sharing

Peer-sharing among "novices" was identified as the main source of support and key enabler in the HEI environment. The four BFNA's written reflections and discussions did not immediately critique the university. Za acknowledged that:

> I was assisted by a colleague . . . in a neighbouring office who was still a novice, a year older than me in HEI. We worked together trying to figure out how the systems work.

Fumza experienced similar challenges to two other Black female academics who were employed a year after her. She shared that the sense of being a "sister's keeper" led her to ask more questions, consult the university website and work closely with university administrators, particularly those within her discipline.

These accounts show that female academics did not wait passively for things to happen, but demonstrated a sense of agency. However, they identified more constraints than enablers of transformation on their arrival in HE.

Thrown in the Deep End

All four BFNA recounted that they felt "thrown in the deep end" on arrival at the university. Yellow-bone and Za explained that the HEI environment, terminology and practices were very different from those in the DoE. Terms and acronyms used in meetings and communication such as cost centers, course modules, Performance Management (PM) and Talent Management (TM) were "confusing."

Some BFNA felt unprepared to develop modules. Kgotsi recalled: "I struggled with developing module outlines; course packs; understanding the requirements of the programme." Others noted that lack of support from sea-soned academics made teaching and learning a challenge. These accounts raise questions about how much HEIs know about so-called "novices."

The Travails of Publication

It is very daunting for "novice" academics to publish in accredited journals and books. Many find the publication process nerve-wracking, emotional and demanding. All four participants were expected to teach, complete their PhDs, supervise at least six Masters' students and publish, among other requirements. Za recalled: "I struggled to launch my research career, and experienced difficulties establishing a publication record because I had limited exposure to and involvement in research activities." Yellow-bone observed that "before PhD qualification, the question would be about your PhD. After graduation and currently the question is: How are the papers and publications coming?"

Unlike the other three participants, Kgotsi was a post-doctoral fellow before she was employed on a full-time basis and had already published three articles. However, on becoming a permanent member of staff, her output diminished and she felt that she was still regarded as a "novice." Fumza also noted that: "I have more than five publications and graduated eleven masters' students . . . but anyway a novice is a novice." This again raises the question of how "novice" is conceptualized in the HEI.

Balancing Family Life and Academia

In reflecting on their family life and their circumstances, as women, society expects BFNA to fulfill certain family responsibilities. Yellow-bone recalled that she was advised to be selfish about her time, as research is the priority and she should make her family understand that. ". . . One cannot save the world." Kgotsi also pointed to misalignment between her domestic responsibilities and the demands of the university. In general, Black female academics have more personal responsibilities than their male Black counterparts. Acknowledging the roles that some female academics have to play should thus be a starting point in understanding the transformation of HEIs.

Our Collective Transformative Journey

Zihlobo has created a safe space to share and reflect on our experiences as BFNA. Embedded in our lived experiences, it has also offered a space to prepare us to change our own lives and act as agents of transformation in HE (Mazibuko, 2006). This includes how we are constructed and various strategies to address our challenges. As Black women academics we must awaken ourselves to what is happening, take action to overcome oppressive conditions and adopt an empowerment model of intervention in order to detach from the "victim syndrome" (Jones, Wilder, & Osborne-Lampkin, 2015; Mazibuko, 2006). By establishing Zihlobo, we took responsibility for transformation by questioning existing support for Black female academics and our different roles, and conceiving the means of transforming our lives as academics.

Post-apartheid education in South Africa has been perceived as a key liberating arena. Zihlobo offers other women and HEIs a useful theoretical perspective to guide their efforts to enhance transformation (Dominguez-Whitehead & Moosa, 2014) and facilitate critical thinking, self-awareness and collective learning. Ebersöhn and Eloff (2006) noted that each community boasts assets, skills and resources that can be linked and maximized to create a more effective community. Zihlobo aims to foreground Black female academics' assets to enable them to become agents of transformation in their own lives, those of their families and HEIs.

Conclusion

This chapter reflected on the Zihlobo initiative and highlighted its value in advancing transformation as individuals and as a collective. It showed that BFNA position themselves not as mere "novices" but as active agents. Alongside other empirical evidence, the Zihlobo experience suggests that social initiatives can be extremely effective in harnessing resources for BFNA and in mitigating some of the challenges they face (Jones et al., 2015). However, ongoing dialogue on formal policies and programmes that aim to support Black female academics is equally important to advance transformation. Given that this is work-in-progress, further exploration of such networks would be worthwhile. Finally, the findings may not be generalizable to a larger population because the data were limited to a few participants from one university.

References

Alexander, N. (2006). *Racial identity, citizenship and nation-building in post-apartheid South Africa*. Retrieved June 18, 2018, from www.marxists.org/archive/alexander/2006-racial-identity-citizenship-and-nation-building.pdf

Badat, S. (2010). *The challenges of transformation in higher education and training institutions in South Africa*. Development Bank of Southern Africa. Retrieved March 6, 2017, from www.dbsa.org/EN/About-Us/Publications

Bartman, C. C. (2015). African American women in higher education: Issues and support strategies. *College Student Affairs Leadership, Grand Valley State University, 2*(2).

Boughey, C. (2007). Educational development in South Africa: From social reproduction to capitalist expansion? *Higher Education Policy, 20*(1), 5–18.

Braun, V., & Clarke, V. (2006). Using thematic analysis in psychology. *Qualitative Research in Psychology, 3*, 77–101.

Bruner, J. (2004). Life as narrative. *Social Research, 71*(3), 691–710.

Chester, E. A., & Espelin, J. M. (2003). Nurture novice educators. *Faculty Issues, 28*(96), 250–254.

Chimanikire, P., Mutandwa, E., Gadzirayi, C. T., Muzondo, N., & Mutandwa, B. (2007). Factors affecting job satisfaction among academic professionals in tertiary institutions in Zimbabwe. *African Journal of Business Management, 1*(6), 66–179.

Cohen, L., Manion, L., & Morrison, K. (2011). *Research methods in education.* Abingdon: Routledge.

Creswell, J. W. (2014). *Research design: Qualitative, quantitative and mixed methods approaches.* Los Angeles, CA: Sage Publications, Inc.

Department of Education. (1997). *Education white paper 3: A programme for the transformation of higher education.* Pretoria: Department of Education.

Department of Education. (2008). *Report of the ministerial committee on transformation and social cohesion and the elimination of discrimination in public higher institutions.* Pretoria: Department of Education.

Department of Higher Education and Training. (2015, October 15–17). *Reflections on higher education transformation.* Discussion paper prepared for the second National Higher Education Transformation Summit, Annexure 5, Universities South Africa.

Dominguez-Whitehead, Y., & Moosa, M. (2014). New academics in the South African research-oriented academy: A critical review of challenges and support structures. *Alternation Special Edition, 12*, 260–282.

Ebersöhn, L., & Eloff, I. (2006). *Life skills & assets* (2nd ed.). Pretoria: Van Schaik Publishers.

Flick, U. (2014). *An introduction to qualitative research* (5th ed.). London: Sage Publications, Inc.

Freire, P. (1973). *Education for critical consciousness.* New York: Continuum Publishing Company.

Goulet, D. (1974). *Introduction.* In P. Freire (Ed.), *Education for critical consciousness.* New York: Continuum Publishing Company.

Higgs, P. (2016). The African renaissance and the transformation of the higher education curriculum in South Africa. *Africa Education Review, 13*(1), 87–101.

Jones, T. B., Wilder, J. A., & Osborne-Lampkin, L. (2015). Beyond sisterhood: Using shared identities to build peer mentor networks and secure social capital in the academy. In B. L. H. Marina (Ed.), *Mentoring away the glass ceiling in academia: A cultural critique* (pp. 143–161). MD: Lexington Books.

Kadi-Hanifi, K. (2013). Black at higher education. *Universal Journal of Educational Research, 1*(2), 83–92. Retrieved February 15, 2017, from www.hrpub.org

Kretzmann, J. P., & McKnight, J. L. (1993). *Building communities from the inside out: A path toward finding and mobilizing a community's assets.* Evanston, IL: Center for Urban Affairs and Policy Research, Northwestern University.

MacDonald, C. (2012). Understanding participatory action research: A qualitative research methodology option. *Canadian Journal of Action Research, 13*(2), 34–50.

Maree, J. G. (2013). *Counselling for career construction. Connecting life themes to construct life portraits: Turning pain into hope.* Rotterdam, The Netherlands: Sense Publishers.

Mazibuko, F. (2006). Women in academic leadership in South Africa: Conventional executives or agents of empowerment. *Alternation, 13*(1), 106–123.

McArthur-Rouse, F. J. (2008). From expert to novice: An exploration of the experiences of new academic staff to a department of adult nursing studies. *Nurse Education Today, 28*(4), 401–408.

Mitchell, C. (2011). *Doing visual research.* London: Sage Publications, Inc.

Naicker, L. (2013). The journey of South African women academics with a particular focus on women academics in theological education. *Studia Historiae Ecclesiasticae, 39,* 325–336.

Quin, L. (2012). *Re-imagining academic staff development: Spaces for disruption.* Stellenbosch: SUN MeDIA- Sun Press.

Remmik, M., Karm, M., Haamer, A., & Lepp, L., (2011). Early-career academics' learning in academic communities. *International Journal for Academic Development, 16*(3), 187–199.

Republic of South Africa. (1996). *Constitution of the republic of South Africa, Act 108 of 1996.* Pretoria: Government Printers.

Swanagan, M. (2014). *Developing a critical consciousness: Black women and the intersection of hair and power* (Master's Thesis Proposal), Published by ProQuest LLC.

Ukpokudu, O. (2010). How a sustainable campus-wide diversity curriculum fosters academic success. *Multicultural Education, 17*(2), 27–37.

Webster, L., & Mertova, P. (2007). *Using narrative inquiry as a research method: An introduction to using critical event narrative analysis in research on learning and teaching.* London, New York: Routledge.

Diverse and Multicultural Teaching

What approaches are being utilized or could be utilized by South African higher education institutions to create and advance diverse and multicultural teaching practices and programming?

5 Is an Agenda for an Inclusivity Framework to Drive Transformation a Possibility or an Idealistic Dream?

Rita Kizito

Introduction

Inclusivity in South African higher education (HE) academic practices for previously marginalized groups is still in an exploratory phase, despite an increase in South African HE transformation research. There are many challenges that present barriers to bringing about meaningful transformation, one of which could be the lack of some type of inclusivity framework. This chapter attempts to address the problem of how to promote marginalized-group inclusivity by borrowing from theories of academic professional identity formation and inclusivity, to analyze accounts of lived experiences of Black women academics from marginalized groups in one South African university in the Eastern Cape. Existing research on marginalized groups tends to focus on finding out how group members respond to current challenges. Very few researchers have approached marginalized group issues from an inclusivity perspective, with the intent of building a cohesive understanding of inclusivity in academic practices. This chapter provides a preview of how this information could be used to develop an inclusivity framework for Black women academics in South African institutions.

Marginalized-group inclusivity seems to be a relatively new concept in the South African HE transformation agenda. Although there have been thorough examinations of the historical experiences of discrimination and marginalization of certain groups, especially Black women academics (Ramohai, 2014), suggestions of how to counteract these destructive practices are limited. The percentage of women enrolled in South African public HE institutions continues to grow. Women constituted 58% of the total headcount enrollment for 2013. Unfortunately, these distributions do not extend to university management data, where women remain under-represented in senior positions (Machika, 2014). Conventional thinking blames the institutional systems for being unable to address marginalized-group concerns. Not enough has been done to consider nuances related to marginalized-group inclusivity during the development of transformation interventions; especially, how *side-lined* group members want to address issues of inclusivity. Thus, there is a need to approach transformation with a knowledge of the strength and limitations of marginalized individuals in mind, and at the same time consider how issues of inclusivity in transformation can be better addressed.

This chapter focuses on seeking ways of describing and categorizing marginalized-group inclusivity for purposes of addressing its ramifications. The emphasis is on the need for designing transformative activities able to thrive within the protected niches of a rather stagnated transformative agenda. Having a set of components for classifying marginalized-group inclusivity to refer to is likely to make the process of designing transformative interventions easier. The aim of this paper is to try to present an Inclusivity Framework as a mechanism that can be used to identify the dimensions and components of meaningful transformation.

Recent research dealing with transformation in South African academic circles points to certain shortcomings. For instance, Nkhumeleni (2012), in her analysis of whether the contributions of South African Research chairs contributed to an acceleration of transformation, found that policy implementation was constrained by the disparity between policy objectives and implementation results. Ramohai (2014) in her study reported that Black women had a negative perception about social transformation. Soudien (2011, p. 15) argued that the reason transformation is not effective is due to "a relative neglect of questions of epistemology and forms of knowledge that fall outside the mainstream Western model." There is little emphasis on the conceptualization of a structure of inclusivity in transformation.

The proposed inclusive framework builds on elements from transformative learning (Mezirow, 2000). Transformative learning is viewed as a developmental progression that involves changing individual identities, reformulating how one *comes to know* by reconfiguring previously held beliefs, worldviews and assumptions as one makes sense of new, filtered experiences in different social milieu. Elements from Critical Race Theory (CRT) (Delgado & Stefancic, 2001) are then juxtaposed onto transformative learning to demarcate a stance on inclusivity. The general view held by CRT scholars is that racism is a persistent source of exclusion and inequality tightly intertwined within the fabric of society. Racism is not the only source of inequality, but it is a dominant source, particularly in the South African context where racism was institutionalized. The use of CRT can help identify disparities related to exclusionary practices, and signpost ways of reducing these disparities. An inclusive framework which combines a developmental forward-leaning approach, with a delineation of existing structural impediments (using CRT), could provide a mechanism for improving inclusivity in academic transformational activities.

This chapter presents an integrative framework that draws on previous research and current practice. First, I introduce the proposed framework. Second, I draw on interview data to describe and illustrate some of the key features of the suggested framework. Lastly, I make recommendations for further research in addressing marginalized-group inclusivity in the transformational agenda.

Inclusivity in Academic Practice

In this section, I describe the two main facets of the proposed inclusive framework, namely: (a) a developmental-oriented approach that draws from transformative learning; (b) Critical Race Theory dimensions that foster inclusivity. Ultimately, the aim is to ensure that each academic can function optimally and is able to "deliver high-quality, engaging education and research" (Debowski, 2012, p. 3). I draw examples from selected literature texts to make key points.

A Developmental-Oriented Approach

The capability of each university academic is regarded as a key factor in ensuring institutional achievement and uniqueness and requires universities to recruit the best academics. In the South African context where there are 55,053 academic staff members employed in the public university sector, it seems disproportionate that only 38.7% are Black. Furthermore, 44.4 % of female candidates are in senior management positions. Of the latter, very few are Black women (CHE, 2018).

In such a context, there is a need to focus on systematic institutional strategies geared at developing Black women's career identities and personal characteristics that will enhance their successful participation. Socioeconomic factors should be factored in, and the physical and mental wellbeing of these academics should also be considered if inclusivity is to be achieved (Machika, 2014; Ramohai, 2014).

Naicker (2013) in her review of the journeys and experiences of women academics draws attention to the precarious position in which Black women academics find themselves. As women, their voices tend to be dismissed and trivialized. In addition, Black women's experiences

> . . . are often overshadowed by the experiences of black men or subsumed under the realities of White women. The universalising of their experiences as black or female does little to affirm their uniqueness and their struggles.
>
> (Naicker, 2013, p. 3)

Principles that address gender issues should be incorporated in transformative plans that are inclusive and affirming (English & Irving, 2012). However, the gender issues should be from Black women's perspectives. There is a need to hear more Black women's voices in both academic and social spaces. This does not preclude collaboration with other women and men.

Building an academic career is becoming increasingly complex in an HE environment which is unpredictable, competitive and constantly changing. Academics are now expected to assume different roles and responsibilities where they are required to teach, design curriculum, work collaboratively, communicate effectively while building and maintaining research track records in their disciplines. Academics are now compelled to assume a scholarly approach to teaching, innovation, research and publishing in the areas of academic practice on top of their disciplinary research (Debowski, 2012). For those who are interested in undertaking senior leadership roles, the added responsibilities and expectations can be overwhelming. For the Black woman academic, who is constantly facing marginalization and exclusion in the HE space, the stakes are even higher.

By utilizing the tenets of Mezirow's (1978) theory of transformative learning as a lens through which experiences are analyzed, Black women academics can be assisted in attaining meaning and balance in academic life within a relatively minimally supportive and somewhat hostile environment. The core elements of transformational learning theory include personal experiences, critical reflection, dialogue, holistic orientation, context and authentic relationships. Mezirow's (2000) view of transformative learning is predominantly individualistic. He inferred that adult learning necessitated the testing of one's assumptions and worldviews, through processes of reflective discourse and critical thinking. This process went beyond the attainment of self-directed learning proposed by Knowles (1989). Although not as radical as Paulo Freire's (1973) emancipatory and social change-induced transformational learning which demands consciousness awareness and raising, Mezirow's transformational learning processes are quite useful for mapping the development of perspective change (see Figure 5.1).

It takes time to embed these processes within a transformative agenda. What is important is the provision of pivotal and scaffolding mechanisms throughout the process that allow the "transformed" individuals to reintegrate into society with transformed perspectives. To facilitate women's transformation, English and Irving (2012) suggest paying attention to five gendered elements:

a. Building relationships by working in groups and fostering mentorships. However, cautionary measures should be taken to ensure that appropriate boundaries are established in the instituted professional relationships.

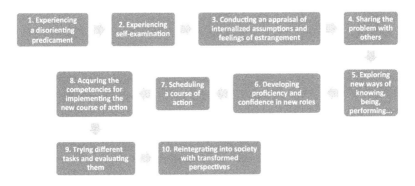

Figure 5.1 Mapping the Development of Perspective Change (Transformative Learning, 2006)

b. The consideration of the centrality of a woman's physical body as demonstrated during periods of menstruation, pregnancy and menopause. A plea is made to consider other forms of learning other than rational cognitive learning.

c. The importance of emotion in transforming one's circumstances (Freire, 1970).

d. The role of creativity and art in effecting transformation. Use of activities such as role plays and storytelling are encouraged.

e. The significance of race and class and their effects on transformation.

These authors' recommendation is that educators and researchers try to combine both strands of transformational learning theory in their practices: ". . . a personally oriented approach," advocated by Mezirow (1978), and ". . . the more global and social justice strain" envisioned by Freire (1970) (English & Irving, 2012, p. 255).

CRT in Transformational Activities

The use of CRT offers an opportunity to investigate the role of race in heightening academic practice injustices. Some architects of CRT such as Delgado and Stefancic (2001) were interested in understanding why racial inequalities persisted despite attempts made to reduce them. Ramohai (2014), on the other hand, uses CRT to analyze the perceived illegitimate deportment of Black women academics in institutional spaces. Both these approaches are consistent with the aims of this chapter, which are to understand how best to reduce barriers that impede Black women academics' efforts to realize their potential.

Although there are some variations among theorists, CRT is guided by five main tenets, according to Solórzano and Yosso (2002). These are: (1) the centrality of race and racism in organizing any society where issues of race are endemic and not marginal; (2) positing a challenge to the dominant, White privilege standpoint is displayed as objective and neutral, while silencing less privileged viewpoints; (3) adopting a transdisciplinary perspective where phenomena are analyzed from both contextual historical and contextual contemporary perspectives; (4) the centrality of experiential knowledge in analyzing and understanding the lived experiences of marginalized communities; and (5) a commitment to social justice and to the provision of transformative responses to inequality and other forms of subordination.

Structural Barriers

There is a persistence of racist practices within HE institutions (Naicker, 2013; Ramohai, 2013; Soudien, 2012). Even after years of calls for transformation, institutions have not been able to adequately address issues of racial disparities and social injustices for Black academics in general, and Black women academics in particular. Traditional norms still hold that women, especially Black women, remain at the lower echelons of the academic ladder. It is not unusual to have the competence of Black women academics questioned (Mokhele, 2013). There are generally lower expectations of Black women (Machika, 2014). Unfortunately, "an institutional culture that privileges white competence and marginalises black competence" (Ramohai, 2014, p. 9) still prevails.

According to Soudien (2011), the South African system has had several initiatives established to address racial disparities. For example, a *Ministerial Committee on Progress towards Transformation and Social Cohesion and the Elimination of Discrimination in Public Higher Education Institutions* was set up after a 2007 incident at the University of the Free State, where four White students ill-treated five Black members of staff. In 2010, the Centre for the Advancement of Non-Racism and Democracy (CANRAD) was established at the Nelson Mandela University (NMU) to encourage non-racial discourses and difficult dialogues that could lead to transformation. The Centre has done remarkable work in addressing racial inconsistencies within NMU. Still, the voices of Black women have been rather muffled in these types of discourses (Ramohai, 2014). When Black women's voices surface, there is a tendency to focus on emboldening individual agency while neglecting to address the systemic structural barriers that perpetuate racial inequality. Women often feel inadequate to express themselves and often, Black male academics dominate these discussions.

Marginalized groups tend to concentrate on their oppression rather than seek to understand why the distributions of cultural power remain unchanged. Freire (2000) argued that this was because the oppressed were trained not to see the structural foundations of their oppression. Agherdien and Pillay (2018) assert that educators need an "understanding of the larger inequalities, power differentials and injustices that are at play within the South African education system" (p. 1) to address prevailing social injustices. Although aimed at student learning, the same assertion works for adult learning and transformation.

The Proposed Inclusivity Framework to Support Transformation

Inclusivity in South African HE academic practices for previously marginalized groups is still in an exploratory phase, despite an increase in South African HE transformation research. There are many challenges that present barriers to bringing about meaningful transformation, one of which could be the lack of some type of inclusivity framework. A complete account of all the facets for all phases of the transformation cycle is outside the scope of this chapter. However, the presentation of a possible inclusivity framework and the preliminary interview data of a Black woman academic using the framework is an attempt to provide some valuable insight into this complex field.

The proposed framework consists of three dimensions (see Figure 5.2):

1. A transformative learning dimension which offers a platform for appraising the status quo of participating academics, providing accounts of their self and cultural identities, past experiences, together with institutional mechanisms for supporting transformation and growth;
2. A CRT dimension which embeds the five CRT tenets;
3. An inclusivity dimension which provides a space for addressing the barriers to inclusivity.

Each dimension in the framework is divided into a few components that can be further investigated and modified in future studies. The combination of dimensions and components can be used to strengthen the framework and later on, to offer a description of the level of inclusivity within an institutional transformational agenda.

The next section provides an illustration of the main ideas of the proposed "inclusivity framework" through a process of scrutinizing of interview data.

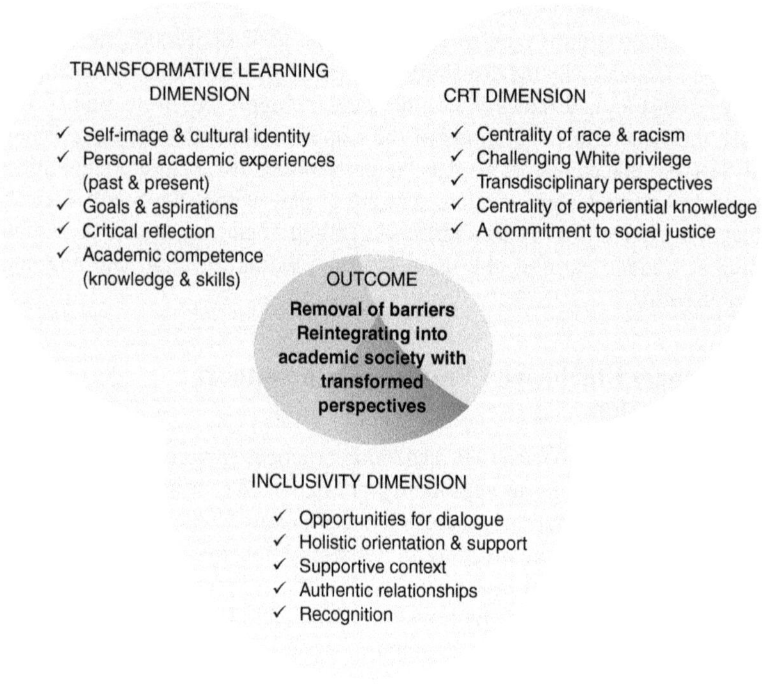

TRANSFORMATIVE LEARNING
DIMENSION

✓ Self-image & cultural identity
✓ Personal academic experiences
  (past & present)
✓ Goals & aspirations
✓ Critical reflection
✓ Academic competence
  (knowledge & skills)

CRT DIMENSION

✓ Centrality of race & racism
✓ Challenging White privilege
✓ Transdisciplinary perspectives
✓ Centrality of experiential knowledge
✓ A commitment to social justice

OUTCOME

**Removal of barriers
Reintegrating into
academic society with
transformed
perspectives**

INCLUSIVITY DIMENSION

✓ Opportunities for dialogue
✓ Holistic orientation & support
✓ Supportive context
✓ Authentic relationships
✓ Recognition

Figure 5.2 Proposed Inclusivity Framework to Support Transformation

Drawing on Interview Data to Illustrate Some Key Features of the Suggested Framework

Study Context

The setting of the study testing the framework was a comprehensive University in the Eastern Cape region of South Africa. The small group of four Black women academics interviewed were selected because they expressed an interest in participating in the study. Three of the staff members had doctoral degrees and were seeking promotion to associate professor level, while one sought promotion to senior lecturer level. Three staff members were from the Education faculty, while the remaining academic was from the Chemistry department (Science Faculty).

A semi-structured interview schedule was used to probe the level of inclusivity as experienced by each academic. The dimensions and components (see Table 5.1) provided a structure for composing the interview questions.

Table 5.1 Dimensions and Components within the Inclusivity Framework

	DIMENSIONS		
	TRANSFORMATIVE LEARNING	*INCLUSIVITY*	*CRT*
COMPONENTS	Self-image & cultural identity	Opportunities for dialogue	Centrality of race & racism
	Personal academic experiences (past & present)	Holistic orientation & support	Challenging White privilege
	Goals & aspirations	Supportive context	Transdisciplinary perspectives
	Critical reflection	Authentic relationships	Centrality of experiential knowledge
	Academic competence (knowledge & skills)	Recognition	A commitment to social justice
	Barriers and resistance to development and progress		

The interviews were transcribed and a constant comparison data analysis method (Glaser, 1965) was used to code and analyze the data in several iterative processes until analytic themes emerged from the data. In this chapter, I present data of one Black woman academic—Dr. Nthabiseng—as an illustration of the struggles and compromises that Black women academics engage with as they seek to rise up the academic career ladder.

Preliminary Findings

Findings are reported under the headings of the three dimensions—transformative learning, CRT and inclusivity.

Transformative Learning Dimension

(a) Dr. Nthabiseng's[1] Background, Goals and Aspirations

Dr. Ntahbiseng is a 60-year-old Black woman academic, born and raised in the Eastern Cape. Currently, she is a well-developed researcher and an experienced academic, but it has taken her longer than the average academic to achieve her dream. She started off as a high school teacher, moved into teacher training before joining the university as an academic developer.

When asked about why she was interested in becoming an academic, here was her response.

> . . . I joined the university because at the school I was teaching I had no prospects for advancing from Head of Department. Besides, my dream from a young age was to become a professor but it has been a struggle, I am almost retiring without achieving that dream.

(b) Dr. Nthabiseng's Graduate Education

Dr. Nthabiseng took it upon herself to enroll for Honours degree in Linguistics. She performed very well and was encouraged to take the Masters programme as well. She was given minimal support to complete these two degrees, and taking them as a part-time student meant that it took her double the time required to complete a full-time degree programme. However, she gained confidence to continue on to the PhD programme as well.

> To complete my two degrees . . . I had to take care of my family, do my work. . . . For my Masters, I was the only Black candidate in my team and often, I felt inadequate . . . in my department there was no Black professor, and none to turn to in real times of need but I gained confidence as I learnt to work hard and believe in myself. . .

The CRT Dimension (*Centrality of Race & Racism; Challenging White Privilege*)

One of the biggest challenges faced was the isolation and assumption that because she was Black, she knew less than her White counterparts. Another drawback was the fact that her White colleagues always banded together to discuss ideas and engaged with each other outside campus hours. She only learnt about these engagements from outside sources. She found solace and comfort in joining a Black union organization on campus.

> For me the greatest setback was the feeling of being "the other." Sometime back . . . I used to travel on a bus with Black colleagues from the townships. We came singing in the bus but the moment we reached the university gate, we stopped singing. It felt as if we were leaving our identities and cultures behind. For that reason, I became a member of the Black union organisation. Throughout my time at the university, the union has helped us address lack of transformation . . . my last promotion would have not succeeded had I not been a member of the union.

Inclusivity Dimension

All four candidates were asked about whether the institutions provided opportunities for supporting the Black women academics. Below are some typical questions asked and Dr. Nthabiseng's responses.

---

1. **Are institutional mechanisms designed to foster inclusivity and collaboration between staff of different races?**
   We have processes and transformation committees in each faculty but these are headed by mostly Black academics. There is hardly any participation from the other racial groups. Usually, they meet and report on incidents that escalate—for example, unfairness in promotion.

2. **Is there a shared value to minimize inequalities of opportunity in your department?**
   No. . . . Staff are too scared to raise these issues in public. I tend to work on my own although sometimes I meet with colleagues from different institutions with whom we share the same challenges.

3. **Do you feel that your work is recognized in the institution?**
   Not all the time . . . recently we were supposed to present our work at a conference. We all sat down and agreed on a way forward. To our surprise, our White colleague decided to go ahead and present her own views and left ours out completely.

Summary and Future Directions

The data analyzed here is by no means conclusive. More academics need to be interviewed if the framework is to be strengthened. The preliminary data presented here indicates that additional work needs to be done to support transformation of South African institutions. This needs to happen on two fronts: at the institutional level where debates around the beliefs and values buttressing transformation and inclusivity need to be resurrected; and at the individual level through the provision of support structures and mechanisms to enhance shifts in academic perspectives around inclusivity and transformation.

The combination of the three dimensions—transformative learning, CRT and inclusivity—provides a common language with which academics from diverse cultures can talk to one another about inclusivity and transformation. This process can be enhanced by using the transformative learning model of professional development to bring about perspective transformation. In addition, the CRT framework can provide structures for addressing issues of race and marginalization.

The findings from this preliminary study are significant in the ongoing development of models of review and development of culture, policy and practice for more inclusive and transformative academic practice. If developed further, the framework could provide a structure with which to conceptualize research around issues of inclusivity and transformation in South African institutions. In other words, an agenda for an Inclusivity Framework to drive transformation is a possibility, and not an idealistic dream.

Note

1 Dr. Nthabiseng is a fictitious name for one of the Black women academics.

References

Agherdien, N., & Pillay, R. (2018). Enabling transformation through socially just critical pedagogies in a health and wellbeing course: A South African case study. *Journal of Human Behavior in the Social Environment, 28*(3), 338–354.

Council on Higher Education. (2018). *VitalStats: Public Higher Education 2016.* Retrieved from https://www.che.ac.za/media_and_publications/monitoring-and-evaluation/vitalstats-public-higher-education-2016

Debowski, S. (2012). *The new academic: A strategic handbook.* UK: McGraw-Hill Education.

Delgado, R., & Stefancic, J. (2001). *Critical race theory: An introduction.* New York: New York University Press.

English, L. M., & Irving, C. J. (2012). Women and transformative learning. *The Handbook of Transformative Learning: Theory, Research, and Practice,* 245–259.

Freire, P. (1970). *Education for critical consciousness.* New York: Continuum Publishing Company.

Freire, P. (1973). *Pedagogy of the oppressed.* New York: The Seabury Press.

Freire, P. (2000). *Pedagogy of the oppressed.* New York: Continuum International Publishing Group.

Glaser, B. (1965). *The constant comparative method of qualitative analysis.* Oxford, UK: Oxford University Press.

Knowles, M. S. (1989). *The making of an adult educator: An autobiographical journey.* San Francisco, CA: Jossey-Bass Inc.

Machika, P. (2014). Mind the gap: The place of women in higher education. *Mail & Guardian.* (Online). Retrieved from http://mg.co.za/article/2014-08-12-mind-the-gap-theplace-of-women-in-higher-education

Mezirow, J. (1978). Perspective transformation. *Adult Education, 28*(2), 100–110.

Mezirow, J. (2000). *Learning as transformation: Critical perspectives on a theory in progress.* San Francisco, CA: The Jossey-Bass Higher and Adult Education Series. Jossey-Bass Publishers, 350 Sansome Way, 94104.

Mokhele, M. (2013). *Reflections of Black women academics at South African Universities: A narrative case study.* Retrieved from https://www.researchgate.net/publication/289862966_Reflections_of_Black_Women_Academics_at_South_African_Universities_A_Narrative_Case_Study

Naicker, L. (2013). The journey of South African women academics with a focus on women academics in theological education. *Studia Historiae Ecclesiasticae, 39,* 325–336.

Nkhumeleni, C. (2012). *The transformation of the higher education institutions in the post-apartheid era: The South African research chairs initiative as an indicator* (Doctoral Dissertation). Pretoria: University of South Africa.

Ramohai, J. (2013). *A living journey towards understanding black women academics' perceptions of social transformation in South African higher education* (Doctoral Dissertation). Bloemfontein, South Africa: University of the Free State.

Ramohai, J. (2013). *A living journey towards understanding black women academics' perceptions of social transformation in South African higher education* (Doctoral Dissertation), University of the Free State.

Ramohai, J. (2014). Marginalised access in South African higher education: Black women academics speak! *Mediterranean Journal of Social Sciences, 5*(20), 2976–2985.

Solórzano, D. G., & Yosso, T. J. (2002). Critical race methodology: Counter-storytelling as an analytical framework for education research. *Qualitative Inquiry, 8*(1), 23–44.

Soudien, C. (2011). The arhythmic pulse of transformation in South African higher education. *Alternation, 18*(2), 15–34.

Soudien, C. (2012). *Realizing the dream: Unlearning of the logic of race in South African schools*. Pretoria: HSRC Press.

Theme 4

Quality Research

What strategies have been introduced or could be introduced in South African higher education institutions to create and advance support for quality research and teaching that benefits the demographic composition of South African academics and students, and the needs of the South African multicultural society?

6 Research Supervision Capacity Building

Towards Sustainable Learning Communities of Practice in South African Higher Education Institutions

Suriamurthee Maistry

Introduction

The Council on Higher Education Vital Stats Report (CHE, 2016) provides unequivocal evidence as to the unevenness of the South African HE terrain. The overall trend indicates that throughput rates continue to range between 30–40%, an alarming statistic that worsens for advanced research degrees (Masters and PhD). The dropout rate is the highest amongst African students, with historically disadvantaged institutions (HDIs) the most affected. African academics still constitute the lowest percentage of PhD qualified staff. In addressing how the nation might advance its research agenda, a somewhat cynical recommendation of the ASSAF Report was that those institutions with established track records should be strengthened (ASSAF, 2010). Of concern was the relative silence on how the research capacity of struggling institutions might be addressed.

In this piece, I reflect on the key issues at play as it relates to novice supervisors in the HE postgraduate supervision context in South Africa (SA). I draw on evidence from having taught on a structured, funded research supervision capacity-building programme at eight HE institutions in SA over the past four years (2015–2018). While each university context and cohort of students was uniquely different and presented with parochial issues, there were certain universal postgraduate supervision challenges, dilemmas, opportunities and constraints that were common across all institutions. In this chapter, I focus on an analysis of the most pertinent issues at play, with a view to theorizing their occurrence and offering tentative insights to engage these issues.

A Brief Note on Methodological Issues. . .

As a pedagogue working in HE, I have come to value the importance of critical reflection on my practice as a teacher. Offering mentorship to young, novice academics and conducting continuing professional development work has in recent years become a core element of the academic work I perform. Regular reflection on the teaching and learning issues that prevail in these multiple, multi-site contexts has enabled me to accumulate a valuable source of "data" (not in the empiricist sense) that I constantly draw on to contribute to and advance the scholarship of teaching in a SA HE context. I draw very specifically on a self-study methodological approach, an appealing, systematic methodology that is fast gaining traction internationally and locally (Pithouse-Morgan & Samaras, 2015). Self-study supports reflective journaling; the construction of narrative accounts/reflections of teaching practice; and a subsequent analysis of key issues as they relate to both the content taught and the recipients of my teaching. The foremost intention is the improvement of one's practice through a dialectic with relevant theory. Critical incidents drawn from my reflections are applied to lead the various arguments that this piece presents.

A Brief Overview of the Strengthening Postgraduate Supervision (SPS) Programme—the Intervention

This programme was the outcome of a joint initiative that included five South African HEIs and three Dutch HEIs. The Netherlands organization for international cooperation in HE (Nuffic) financed the initial development of the programme. The programme is registered as an official course offering at Rhodes University, and is thus subject to the quality assurance protocols of Rhodes University. The course is pitched at NQF level 8, carrying 30 credit points and is designed to run over three distinct phases. Phase 1 is an intensive, structured face-to-face taught component that runs over three days and is usually taught by two facilitators. This is followed by a structured online programme over six to eight weeks, guided by a facilitator. The third and final phase is a three-day face-to-face taught component. The teaching team comprises a pool of experienced and established researchers from various HEIs in SA and the Netherlands. Since its inception, there has been enthusiastic take up at several institutions across the country. Course evaluations indicate that the programme has been well received.

Facilitating this course at eight HEIs, six of which were HDIs, was an "educational" experience as it allowed me to observe firsthand the rich tapestry that is the SA postgraduate arena. Of particular significance is the effect on the agents that have to give effect to national and institutional policy, namely, the HE academics whose research related expectations have altered substantially. This chapter therefore focuses on the "condition" of the novice supervisors as they negotiate their way through the milieu of the postgraduate supervision enterprise.

The ASSAF Report (2010) revealed major challenges including supervisor competence as a key factor in student attrition in HE. A contributing factor is that historically, postgraduate supervision workshops and courses invariably focused on technical policy and administrative aspects of supervision (liberal pre-occupations), seldom considering the likelihood that such supervisory practice might result in social exclusion and student dropout. To its credit the SPS course being reported on engages the notion of *supervision as pedagogy* and *mentorship* and draws on scholarship from the post-liberal realm.

In a context such as SA, which enrolls students with widely varying levels of preparedness for advanced PhD study, research supervision envisaged as a humanizing pedagogy (Khene, 2014) can potentially redirect the focus of supervision so that it centers on the development of the PhD student. The supervision enterprise becomes a matter of managing the tension between the instrumentalist dimension (performance), namely helping students acquire the qualification, and the affective competence dimension, that is nurturing students' "self-development, academic identity, self-worth and growth" (Wisker, 2012, p. 6). Lee (2008) argues that while a functional approach to postgraduate supervision has value, a conceptual approach involving enculturation into a disciplinary community, critical thinking and emancipation through self-development are also important elements of the supervision enterprise. The challenge is to determine how to help move novice supervisors towards achieving high-level research supervision competence.

In this chapter, I examine key issues at play in the postgraduate research supervision capacity development arena in the SA context by illuminating the fractures and fault lines at work as well as the opportunities and potential for advancing this aspect of the HE mandate. I focus specifically on the lived realities and wellbeing of novice "chalkface" academics as they contend with the multiple demands that comes with teaching and research in HE.

Drowning in Teaching and Administration: A Profound Sense of Despair!

A key theme in the SPS programme is the examination of the context within which supervision takes place. A striking feature at every institution, as reflected in the nature and content of the commentary by the participants, is the level of overt depression that has beset the HE landscape in SA. This mental state is evident in the hopelessness discourse that prevails, the sense of being overwhelmed by multiple competing demands, the kind that derives from the schizophrenic nature of many SA HEIs (Maistry, 2012). Shore refers to this phenomenon as the multiple personality disorder university (Shore, 2010), a state in which chalk-face academics encounter confounding objectives. A common challenge indicated at almost every institution was the inordinate amount of time spent on teaching and administration. Teaching remains the core pedagogic activity of especially new, young academics, also burdened with administration of large classes. This drains personal physical and emotional energy and results in perennial fatigue. Such junior colleagues are usually at the mercy of often unsympathetic line managers. The plight of such colleagues is compounded when research supervision is tagged on to their workloads.

In many instances, such colleagues held coursework Masters degrees. When thrust into the research supervision arena, many find the prospect of supervising Masters students particularly daunting. Of particular concern is that in almost all cases, no attempt was made to assess such colleagues' competence to supervise at this level. As relative newcomers to their academic communities, they struggle to induct their new students into the discourses and ways of thinking and being in such communities, a competence they themselves have not mastered (Maistry, 2017). When postgraduate research supervision is academically unsound and expedient, multiple risks are likely to ensue.

At many institutions, there is no policy/guidelines on how to "measure" or establish the time needed to effectively supervise postgraduate students. While I loathe the neoliberal move to quantify the rich work of university academics, in this instance, where the burden has become excessive and to a large extent "ignored" by disconnected university managers, such quantification might well help to foreground the plight of the contemporary South African academic. For institutions where such conversations have not yet started, it might well prove a productive move to learn from other institutions that have developed workload models. Deep skepticism of such quantification should however always be an imperative. Low morale and a self-deprecating discourse were common features at many institutions where this SPS programme was run. As such, the disruption of such self-censure discourses and feelings of hopelessness (and helplessness) was a real issue that course facilitators had to deal with.

The Risks with Unsolicited Supervision and Random Pairings of Novice Supervisor and Student

When postgraduate supervision is foisted upon academics, it is not unusual to expect that the supervision enterprise has potential to become a highly fraught encounter. It is cause for serious concern when supervisors enter into the supervision relationship as reluctant, angry and coerced by systems they cannot challenge. On the negative, the underprepared, heavy teaching workload-burdened academic, enters the relationship unwillingly and often grudgingly. Unsuspecting students, expecting high-level supervision from astute academics with a full repertoire of research supervision competences, are likely to be short changed. This HE supervision challenge is acute in SA but not peculiar to this context, as Manathunga and Gozee remind us that this is also a global problem (Manathunga & Gozee, 2007).

The SA context is characterized by a disproportionate number of under-qualified academics; in excess of 60% not holding a PhD qualification (ASSAF, 2010). Such individuals are under enormous pressure to enroll for PhD study as well as to develop and maintain a conferencing and publication profile. As can be expected, levels of anxiety and insecurity are pervasive as desperate novice academics scramble to "please" their masters in order to keep their jobs and establish credibility. Often, out of ignorance and naivety, individuals accept and supervise students in focal areas outside of their immediate field of (limited) expertise. This situation is largely the outcome of institutions' quest to meet inflated enrollment targets; a condition where anybody and everybody who meets a dubious minimum entrance requirement is accepted into high-level postgraduate study. Risk becomes layered and complex and manifests at different levels. It can be argued that remaining at the "cutting edge" of research and active debates in one's own disciplinary field, while stimulating, is in itself an arduous and time-consuming task. It follows then that attempting to enter and gain sophisticated understandings of contemporary deliberations in "foreign" disciplines might well prove elusive and immensely frustrating. The consequence is that the novice supervisor precariously relies on the research student to adequately master this "foreign" theoretical (and methodological) terrain.

How then might the emerging academic navigate what might be perceived as a perilous, complex research enterprise both as novice researcher and supervisor? In the section that follows, I examine the potential that a "community of practice" approach might offer, by drawing on the seminal work of social theorist Etienne Wenger (Wenger, 1999).

Towards Building a Community of Practice

As described above, the SPS course has had very positive uptake at HDIs. A significant feature of all institutions was the absence of active collegial networks where novice and experienced supervisors could engage in deliberations on the postgraduate research enterprise. Although all institutions had Research/Higher Degrees committees, these were much more formal spaces where routine administrative and procedural postgraduate business was conducted, including the vetting of research proposals and the appointment of examiners. These committees were usually inhabited by senior academics. As such, intimate institutional knowledge as it relates to postgraduate research, policies and procedures remains in a somewhat constricted domain as opposed to its wider dispersal especially amongst new supervisors.

In some instances, public defense of proposals before small committees did in fact take place. Here again, the formality and evaluative nature of engagement in such a space is likely to introduce unnecessary strain on the research learning process. Many participants indicated that their "learning to be a supervisor" was regrettably limited to their own experience as student. This thus begs the question as to how, when, where and with whom novice supervisors (also novice PhD researchers themselves) might learn the art and craft of research supervision. How might such spaces develop organically as opposed to contrived formations that might have limited sustainability? How might "natural" communities of practice germinate? In an insightful book entitled *Cultivating Communities of Practice: A Guide to Managing Knowledge* (Wenger, McDermott, & Snyder, 2002), a comprehensive account of how a community of practice might function in a work environment is presented.

In offering a structural model of a community of practice, Wenger et al. (2002) suggested that such communities comprise three fundamental elements, namely, a *domain, community* and *practice*. The *domain* refers to the core business or common enterprise that defines or circumscribes the identity of the community of practice. It serves to inspire its members to be active contributors, guides learning and gives meaning to the work of the community. The community decides the agenda. As the work of the community proceeds, members become involved in the development of a practice (Wenger et al., 2002). In applying the concept of domain to communities of practice in HE postgraduate research and supervision, one might venture that varying domains might well prevail.

Community is referred to as the creation of the "social fabric of learning" (Wenger et al., 2002, p. 28) where regular interactions and valuable relations are fostered based on mutual trust and respect. Learning is a matter of belonging and participation is entirely voluntary. Such communities might comprise varying numbers of participants, but it relies on a critical mass to sustain its existence. A community of practice's prolonged existence is more likely if there is a degree of distributed internal leadership. Its success is a function of the productive energy that it can generate. While recognized experts bring credibility to its work, such individuals may not necessarily be the "glue" that brings the community together. The culture of every community will differ as will the level of intensity of the engagement. The emphasis however is always on collective inquiry and learning (Wenger et al., 2002).

Practice represents a "set of frameworks, ideas, tools, information, styles, language, stories, and documents that community members share" (Wenger et al., 2002, p. 29). It refers to shared, accepted protocols and action that give rise to the knowledge and skills that the community constructs and maintains. Wenger et al. maintain that the hallmark of a healthy community of practice is when all three elements (domain, community and practice) function as a cohesive whole.

Three domains that might have immediate and direct relevance for novice postgraduate supervisors present themselves. Firstly, a domain that focusses on discipline-specific issues. Mathematics for example could have participants engaged with the disciplinary discourse, conventions, writing, and thinking and the engagement with historical and contemporary Mathematics disciplinary knowledge. The same would apply to communities of practice in Physics, Psychology, Law, etc.

Secondly, a domain that emphasizes the object of supervision as pedagogy is another possibility. Here the focus could be on very specifically engaging theories and practices of research supervision, very much in line with the supervisory issues covered in the SPS course described above. The SPS course and its consequent "recruitment" of novice supervisors was one such community of practice that seeded at each institution. A significant enabling factor is the organic formation of a core group that take on the leadership of the community, encouraging, motivating, disseminating information and importantly, active engagement with the key enterprise of the community which in this instance was the learning of supervision as a pedagogy.

The third possible domain, and arguably the most powerful, is a community in which both disciplinary deliberations on cutting edge issues as well as research are engaged with as an integrated composite. In communities like this, the novice academic is exposed to contemporary debates in their specific field through regular interactions with both novice and established scholars in their field. Reading groups and journal clubs have proven to be productive spaces where much collaborative learning can happen (Golde, 2007). The research aspect of this domain becomes much more pointed and might focus on latest methodological issues and developments in the field. It could also include pertinent aspects as it relates to disciplinary and institutional supervisory practices.

The potential for different kinds of learning for the academic is likely to be exponential once this kind of community of practice develops its rhythm (Wenger et al., 2002). It is very likely that this learning space is where the signature pedagogy of the discipline is learnt (Shulman, 2005). Crucial knowledge which many academics "stumble upon" can be addressed in this forum. A common feature across all institutions where the SPS programme was conducted was the level of ignorance of the resources available to academics to support their research work. Issues such as benchmarks for postgraduate research at different levels, examination policies and processes (including the politics of such processes), peer adjudication processes and funding possibilities are some of the learning possibilities that could emerge in a dynamic, vibrant, disciplinary research community of practice.

In applying the agricultural metaphor of cultivating a community of practice, the pertinent issue is to establish the conditions for the germination of such a community. The first step in this direction is for agents who identify the need to initiate moves towards giving effect to the conceived idea. In this instance, the idea is bringing together a group of novice and inexperienced research supervisors, framing a domain that has appeal to the potential participants and securing experts that will lead the work of the community. As described above, the research office at each participating institution identified and invited novice supervisors to enroll for this programme. The structure of the programme was provided and potential participants had to commit to involvement in all three phases. As mentioned above, the SPS course is on offer as a "taught" programme via Rhodes University. The research office of the target university in collaboration with the co-ordinators at CHERTL (Centre for Higher Education Teaching and Research at Rhodes University) carry out the logistical arrangements. This is a crucial aspect as it determines whether the community of practice actually gets off the ground or not. Particular attention has to be given to the timing. In this instance three days had to be identified for the Phase 1 and Phase 3 contact sessions. These were full day (08h00–16h00) contact sessions. Phase 2 of the course is an online encounter in which participants engage with course activities directed at meeting the course outcomes. This phase could span between six and eight weeks. Given that there is seldom a "quiet" period in any university's academic calendar and the nature of the workload of many participants, this had to be carefully negotiated with the potential participants. Creating the conditions for ease of entry into the community is crucial. The securing of appropriate, comfortable, conducive venues was important as the Phase 1 and 3 contact sessions were full day, intensive programmes. In some cases participating institutions strategically selected venues that were off campus as a way of minimizing distractions that might present if the programme was run on site where work related demands might compromise participants' undivided focus and concentration. In all instances, provision was made for basic sustenance. Scheduled tea breaks and lunch breaks were powerful spaces where participants socialized with one another and the facilitators.

My experience of facilitation of the programme on 15 different occasions, at various universities across the country since 2015, is that each new cohort (even from the same institution) presents with peculiar challenges and opportunities. As facilitator, I have developed a deeper understanding of the extent of the issues faced by academics across the country, especially as it relates to the level of insecurity that many experience. For many, their sense of self-worth and their own assessment of their ability to become a successful academic is alarmingly low. As facilitator, I have had to maintain a heightened sensitivity to these dynamics at play, especially in cohorts where participants were completely new to each other. It became a matter of carefully reading the verbal and non-verbal cues that manifested in each group. The aim was to create the conditions for active, productive participation in an inclusive environment.

As can be expected, the extent of participation and the pace at which trust between the participants and the facilitators developed, varied at each institution. In all instances, there was a need to constantly encourage, cajole and sometimes firmly remind participants of their commitment. Phase 2, the online phase, was particularly challenging for participants as work pressures often frustrated the attempts of many participants to fully engage with all the Phase Two activities. At each institution though, a core group of participants did sustain engagement and regularly posted their contributions to the online communal space. This usually triggered other participants to also share their deliberations. Wenger reminds us that in any community of practice, a core group of participants are usually most active (Wenger, 1999). A discernible feature was the spontaneous constructive online engagements that occurred. In line with the organic nature of any community of practice, participants move between the core and the periphery as and when they see/do not see value in the work of the community. Natural attrition is a feature of any community of practice. The reasons for the attrition ranged from illness to resignations to time constraints.

By Phase 3 of the programme at each institution, it was clear that distinct collegial bonds and friendships had started to form. Wenger notes that a sign that a community of practice has taken root is when members develop a sense of camaraderie, when members begin to operationalize a common language, a peculiar discourse, when they develop a shared repertoire (Wenger, 1999). Of most significance though is when members actively take responsibility for each other's learning. This is arguably the defining moment—when members begin to recognize each other as valuable resources, when members affirm each other's emerging competence and realize how their own growth and learning is intricately and intimately connected to the learning of others.

This revelation and recognition is indeed an epiphany for many participants as it marks the point at which a conscious awareness of a sense of belonging develops, a first real comprehension of being part of a collective. In comprehending and apprehending the domain of the community of practice, and in actively contributing, members move beyond the realm of individual and begin to recognize themselves as bona fide members. It must be noted that a community of practice did in fact form at each of the institutions where the SPS programme was administered, though not in the organic sense that Wenger alluded to.

Conclusion

From the above discussion, it becomes clear that a conceptual understanding of how communities of practice are conceived is useful, as it offers a heuristic for deliberative interventions especially in contexts where the need for the acquisition of strategic competences is exigent. Developing postgraduate research supervision competence is one such exigence that might be meaningfully addressed in communities of practice. Of particular importance in the SA HE context is the extent to which decisive, efficient planning on the part of university research leadership can/is willing to create the conditions that will accelerate the formation of such learning communities.

While the communities of practice framework holds much promise for developing high-level research supervision skills, one needs to be guarded about not over-romanticizing its potential. Arguably the most serious risk to any community of practice is its sustainability. One might well ask what might be the immediate consequences when the expert, the programme facilitator in this instance, exits the community, a salient point worth examining (Maistry, 2017).

What the SPS initiated postgraduate supervision communities of practice have revealed is that enormous learning possibilities present when such communities do get started. Participants indicated that a positive outcome of their involvement in the programme was the stimulus effect it had on their own development as well as the subsequent harnessing of local departmental (disciplinary) energies towards the formation of interest groups such as journal clubs, and other collective research learning spaces. For participants who had never encountered HE research on postgraduate supervision in particular, the exposure to empirical research and theory in this field was indeed a new positive and productive experience.

In essence then, one can surmise that an "extraordinary" effort is required if we wish to address transformation in the HE sector, especially as it relates to developing the research supervision capacity of inexperienced postgraduate supervisors. The SPS programme and the communities of practice that formed at each institution have contributed to South Africa's transformation agenda. The programme was in fact a direct response to a social justice concern, namely the under-preparedness of novice supervisors for the high-level task of research supervision. At another level, it can be rightly argued that because one of the key themes embedded in the programme's content is "social inclusionary" research supervision as it relates to, amongst others, race, gender and sexuality, the transformative agenda was certainly an imperative that was addressed through the programme.

References

ASSAF. (2010). *The PhD study*. Pretoria, South Africa: ASSAF.

Council on Higher Education. (2016). *CHE vital stats: Public higher education*. Pretoria, South Africa: Council on Higher Education.

Golde, C. M. (2007). Signature pedagogies in doctoral education: Are they adaptable for the preparation of education researchers? *Educational Researcher, 36*, 344–351.

Khene, C. P. (2014). Supporting a humanizing pedagogy in the supervision relationship and process: A reflection in a developing country. *International Journal of Doctoral Studies, 9*, 73–83.

Lee, A. (2008). How are doctoral students supervised? Concepts of doctoral research supervision. *Studies in Higher Education, 33*(3), 267–281. doi: 10.1080/03075070 802049202

Maistry, S. M. (2012). Confronting the neoliberal brute: Reflections of a higher education middle-level manager. *South African Journal of Higher Education, 26*(3).

Maistry, S. M. (2017). Betwixt and between: Liminality and dissonance in developing threshold competences for research supervision in South Africa. *South African Journal of Higher Education, 31*(1), 119–134.

Manathunga, C., & Gozee, J. (2007). Challenging the dual assumption of the "always/already" autonomous student and effective supervisor. *Teaching in Higher Education, 12*(3), 309–322.

Pithouse-Morgan, K., & Samaras, A. P. (Eds.). (2015). *Polyvocal professional learning through self-study research*. Rotterdam: Sense Publishers.

Shore, C. (2010). Beyond the multiversity: Neoliberalism and the rise of the schizophrenic university. *Social Anthropology, 18*(1), 15–29.

Shulman, L. S. (2005). Signature pedagogies in the professions. *Daedalus, 134*(3), 52–59.

Wenger, E. (1999). *Communities of practice: Learning, meaning and identity*. New York: Cambridge University Press.

Wenger, E., McDermott, R., & Snyder, W. M. (2002). *Cultivating communities of practice: A guide to managing knowledge*. Boston: Harvard Business School Press.

Wisker, G. (2012). *The good supervisor: Supervising postgraduate and undergraduate research for doctoral theses and dissertations* London: Palgrave Macmillan.

Theme 5

New Institutional Identities

What new institutional identities have been developed or could be developed by merged and non-merged higher education institutions in South Africa to rise above preceding apartheid injustices?

7 Supporting Academic and Social Transformation in a Teacher Education Lecture Room

Ansurie Pillay

Introduction

This chapter reports on a case study involving student teachers of literature in a teacher education programme in the School of Education, University of KwaZulu Natal, who used literary texts as catalysts for implementing transformation. The students were registered for a four-year Bachelor of Education degree, and on completion, they could teach at a school English as a home language or English as a second language. While the requirements of the degree asserted sound disciplinary knowledge and effective pedagogical skills, there was an unrecognized need for an understanding of how to bring about academic and social transformation in the school classrooms in which these students would work, irrespective of context or resources.

Critical pedagogy served as the theoretical framework for the study, which was characterized by interventions using literary texts, within six participatory action research (PAR) cycles over two years. The six literary texts included two novels, two plays, and two films. These texts were: the novel *The Madonna of Excelsior* by Zakes Mda (2002)—based on the real-life events surrounding the arrest of 19 citizens in 1971 rural Free State, South Africa, under the Immorality Act (Immorality Act No. 21 of 1950), which forbade sexual relations between people of different races; *The God of Small Things* by Arundhati Roy (1997)—a novel set in Kerala, India, which tells of the childhood experiences of a set of twins who bear the brunt of those who do not follow society's rules; the play *Sophiatown* by The Junction Avenue Theatre Company (1988)—a South African play, which tells of forced removals in apartheid South Africa (Native Resettlement Act No. 19 of 1954); *The Tempest* by William Shakespeare (1623)—a play of magic, illusion and usurpation of power, and the ramifications of each; the film, *The Colour of Paradise*, directed by Majid Majidi (1999), which tells the story of a young Iranian boy who was physically blind, yet unhindered, and his father, who is blind to the many possibilities in his life; and *Much Ado about*

Nothing, a film based on the play by William Shakespeare and directed by Kenneth Branagh (1993), which tells the story of love returned and unrequited, and the trickery involved in both.

The study was guided by the question: What strategies may be used in a teacher education lecture room in South Africa to empower student teachers with the knowledge, skills and abilities to bring about academic and social transformation and contribute successfully to the educational context within and beyond the classroom?

Theoretical Framework

This study was underpinned by critical pedagogy, which advocates for dialogue and conscientization to develop critical social consciousness (Freire, 1999). In an educational institution, the use of dialogue is aimed at empowering students through engaging with and confronting the prevailing educational discourse. Dialogue and enquiry underpin reflection and action, using a problem-posing approach to education. The relationship of students to teacher is dialogical and each contributes and receives in the educational experience. Conscientization is the means by which students gain an awareness of the experiences that influence their lives and realize their abilities to repeat or transform them (Darder, Baltodano, & Torres, 2009). Thus, education is a catalyst for academic and social transformation, and students may potentially become "transformative intellectuals" (Giroux, 1988, p. 122), who might transform their students in turn.

For students to embrace strategies to bring about academic and social transformation, they must be open to questioning existing norms and learning how to take a stance (Giroux & McLaren, 1996). They have to resist being technicists who transmit knowledge (Giroux, 2009) and, instead, must critically examine the world and the processes that maintain social inequalities, and then work towards transforming them (Apple, 1989). In the current study, students were encouraged to examine knowledge to ascertain how it represents, misrepresents, marginalizes or mediates particular views and social realities.

Giroux (2009) suggests that teachers enable students to draw on their diverse voices and histories as the basis for engaging with and interrogating the various experiences they will encounter. In terms of the curriculum, McLaren (2009) urges teachers to be aware of the way narratives, portrayals and representations in textbooks and literary texts, curriculum materials and social relations found in classroom practices advantage dominant groups and disadvantage subordinate ones. Ultimately, teachers using a critical pedagogy aim to build a society based on non-exploitative relations and social justice. Once the affirmative nature of critical pedagogy is established, it becomes possible for students who have been conventionally voiceless to learn how to critically examine the role society has played in their lives and how to enable the transformation of themselves and others.

Methodology

A qualitative case study, using a critical paradigm, was utilized in a system of interventions with a spiral of six PAR cycles over two years. PAR is a process that brings together "action and reflection, theory and practice, in participation with others, in the pursuit of practical solutions to issues of pressing concern to people" (Reason & Bradbury, 2006, p. 1). The literary texts mentioned earlier were used as interventions to equip students with the knowledge, skills and abilities to bring about academic and social transformation within and beyond the classrooms in which they will teach. From individual interviews with 10 student teachers, and focus groups comprising 8 student teachers, a smaller purposive sample was chosen (Patton, 2002). Students were chosen in terms of race and gender to achieve representativeness of the demographics of the total population in the lecture room, and represented insights from various perspectives on the issues of academic and social transformation. While the primary site of the study was the English Education lecture room, all written work, individual interviews and focus groups occurred outside lecture times. After each cycle, two or more of the following qualitative data generation strategies (focus groups, interviews, student evaluations and written work) were used to explore experiences, evaluate the interventions and answer the research question. Data was analyzed using thematic analysis (Patton, 2002). Ethical clearance was sought and participants were guaranteed anonymity, confidentiality and voluntary participation.

Findings and Discussion

While many findings emerged from the study, for the purposes of this chapter, only certain findings will be considered.

An Enabling Environment to Engage with Strategies for Transformation

Results show that students enjoyed the lectures, and their comfort with participation in class improved as they progressed from cycle to cycle. For example, after cycle one, the majority (83%) felt a sense of uncertainty about their levels of comfort with participating in an interactive class, and in cycle two, a majority of the students (90%) indicated a level of comfort with participation. During the focus group discussions after cycle two, students indicated that they were comfortable talking in the English Education lecture room with one saying, "This is the only class I talk in." When asked for reasons, she answered, "You say, Try. Get it wrong. You get us to try and no one laughs if it's not right." The comments indicated that the students experienced a sense of trust and respect in the class and perceived the lecture room to be a safe place to share their views, affirming Boler's (2004) idea that, for learning to take place, spaces have to be created for all voices to participate with respect.

To study *Sophiatown* in cycle three, role-plays, storytelling, music, poetry and newspaper articles were used to enable a level of comfort when participating. The strategies were designed to engage with issues of race, class, gender and identity. In the individual interviews, students indicated that the co-operative, interactive strategies could prove very powerful in their own classrooms. Through all the cycles, interactive strategies within an enabling environment allowed for issues surrounding transformation to be foregrounded. By the final cycle, students noted in individual interviews that, through the interactive co-operative learning strategies, they had built relationships, had learned to respect each other's views, enjoyed working in pairs and perceived a sense of trust in the lecture room. Of importance for me was the realization that it was imperative to explicitly assure students of respect to ensure comfortable participation, and thus open up pathways for engagement with strategies for transformation. I also needed to encourage students to ask questions and challenge assumptions to advance active engagement and dialogue, an important component of critical pedagogy (Freire, 1999). Thus, a non-threatening, co-operative environment is integral to thinking and reflecting during collaborative activities and to enabling academic and social transformation.

Using Strategies to Respond Critically and Empathetically

If students are to be empowered to bring about academic and social transformation, they need to be able to respond both critically and empathetically to situations and issues. During cycle two, dealing with *The Colour of Paradise*, students worked closely with the film and critiques of the film to engage with issues of tolerance and resilience. During the cycle, they were asked to engage collaboratively with the following question: Is Hashem a good father?

Findings revealed varying responses, with some condemning Hashem for his callous treatment of his son and others understanding why he behaved the way he did. Responses indicated, "He's a good father. He gives them food and a house"; "How can a father be ashamed of his son?" and "He is typical of so many people who worry about what others will say." The comments revealed that students were considering issues and characters from various angles, and that many of them were able to experience empathy by putting themselves in another's shoes. They were thus judging events and choices in the film, and were considering the multiple perspectives presented (Ciardiello, 2004).

After the cycle, they were given a written task that went beyond the storyline:

> *As a teacher, you have to aim for academic and social transformation in your classrooms. What aspects of* The Colour of Paradise *would you focus on to achieve this aim?*

This individual task elicited many questions they would pose to learners, such as: "Despite your biases towards others, how would you feel if you were in their situation?"; "When life gets difficult, how do we cope?"; "Why do we treat people who are different to us differently?"; and "How would you feel if you were blind? How would you feel if you had a blind child?" Thus, they were identifying issues of difference, perseverance and empathy to initiate ideas of change in their classrooms.

Results showed a focus on children's rights and needs: "Children must know what is acceptable and what they need as children. A child's basic rights and needs have to be respected." Another quoted South Africa's Bill of Rights with, "Held in the Bill of Rights is the equality clause and this must be promoted. If any great change is going to take place in our country, we must begin to accept that just because someone is different does not make them any less of a person, whether it's race, religion, gender or disability. I would hold discussions with learners about these issues." The written tasks elicited responses that indicated that they had a good idea of how to use the film to develop sensitivity to issues (Henning, 1993), and how to start critical engagement with issues of change, and helping learners develop academically and socially.

Confronting Transformation

While many strategies were used to engage the students and enable them to interrogate their roles in transforming the educational landscape, it became evident that I needed to confront issues of transformation with them. While I assumed, probably unfairly, that the students would work out how to apply information explored in the lectures to their classrooms, the student evaluations after cycle one indicated a majority were "unsure" about how to use ideas from the lecture room to effect transformation in their classrooms. However, they did note that the writing tasks in pairs were useful to clarifying their thinking and for thinking deeply on their roles and functions. For this reason, it was collaboratively decided that writing tasks would be used more frequently.

A focus group held after cycle two were asked: How can you use literary texts to help your learners develop academically and socially? Students responded, "Talk to them about the issues in the film"; "Get them to discuss, share opinions, debate"; "Ask questions to make them think"; "They have to relate issues to their own lives and to the world." Finally, a student stated, "If we want learners to develop in their school work and in the world, I have to know them. So, find out about their lives, and then build from there." Thus, the students were able to consider possible answers on how to enable transformation.

In cycle three, dealing with *Sophiatown*, role-plays were enacted in pairs and from their desks, thus, not performance-oriented. Unpacking how the pedagogy could be used in their classrooms and how to interrogate issues in the classroom was done explicitly. The interviews after cycle three indicated that they felt, "very confident to deal with issues"; "quite clear about how to use the text to engage with important issues"; and "more on top of things in helping to make a change to learners' lives." The use of explicit teaching proved successful for the class, along with clear pointers about how the issues and events in the play could help to effect academic and social change.

By the end of cycle three, I recognized critical reflection in the students who noted that some of the shorter writing tasks given to them were "fun," and did not help in clarifying and deepening their thinking about transformation. While this recognition was in itself credible, it showed that I had privileged collaboration over critical engagement, and this had to be remedied. It also revealed that students wanted to engage with issues beyond the surface level, an aspect I had failed to recognize.

In cycle four, working with *The God of Small Things*, we worked closely with the text, and used paired work to draw on newspaper articles and an interview with the author to engage with issues of race, caste, gender, identity, tolerance and resilience. Students were also asked to engage with the following question:

> *This novel contains issues that might be considered controversial or uncomfortable. How would you handle such issues should they arise from the literature you teach your learners?*

Their responses comprised three themes: facing issues head on; avoiding issues that were considered controversial or uncomfortable; and focusing on the characteristics of the class, without answering the question. Eighteen students noted that they would face issues head on. A student noted, "Learners must practice making decisions and the classroom must be a safe place where they can speak freely about controversial issues." Another indicated, "When we talk about controversial or uncomfortable issues, learners must be encouraged to contribute and must know that their unique contributions are valued." The students seemed aware that there is a need to move away from Anstey and Bull's (2006) finding that in schools, learners are socialized and controlled into working out what the "correct" answers are supposed to be. Like the students, Kudlick (1999) encourages teachers to establish a class-room based on trust and respect so that learners are empowered to contribute freely. Thus, the above students knew how to confront issues in the text to enable transformation.

Eight students indicated that they would avoid the issues because some issues "make learners uncomfortable"; "are best left for parents to discuss." One asked, "Is it our jobs to show learners those things?" Thus, their com-ments indicated that they intend imposing their values on learners regarding levels of acceptability, the roles and functions of teachers and parents, and perceived outcomes of engaging with controversial or uncomfortable issues. Another shared, "I will allow discussion on certain issues, but I will stop learners when they start discussions that are beyond them. They must know what's acceptable in the classroom." The comments indicate conflicting responses. While discussion would be allowed, only certain issues would be acceptable. While learners would be asked to share views, the teacher needed to control what was acceptable, and certain issues would be avoided. As hooks (2009) notes, teachers cannot claim to encourage freedom of expres-sion while, at the same time, silencing, censoring and suppressing views.

Twelve student teachers focused on the characteristics of the classroom to determine their actions. They noted, for example, that "the discussion of race would be sensitive in a mixed race classroom"; "some things can't be discussed with young learners"; "we need to be careful what we say to girls and boys regarding gender"; and "we have to be aware of the economic status of learners before we assume things." While they were aware of the impor-tance of knowing who their learners were (Giroux, 2009), they did not deal with the question asked of them and instead pointed to the determinants that shaped the discussion process. In many ways, they avoided confronting the question. The responses needed to be unpacked and discussed in the lecture room, and while alternative ways of acting were presented, it is not certain how students will behave in their classrooms. What is important is that the conversation has been opened up.

In cycle five, dealing with the film, *Much Ado about Nothing*, besides working closely with the film, the class engaged with film clips, film critiques and debates on issues of gender and patriarchy. The focus group interview revealed that they could use issues to help learners to transform. A student noted that she would ask learners to consider "how Branagh decided to depict the characters." Another added, "How do you not talk about the abuse in the film? We can't tell learners that abuse has no consequences." A third added, "I look at it now and say, there's more. We must deal with it in our classes. Otherwise, what's the point?" These and other responses indicated that they were able to highlight social justice issues, how authors characterize issues and endorse particular views (Johnson & Freedman, 2005), and how portrayals and representations in texts advantage certain groups (Habermas, 1972). Additionally, a student revealed, "This whole study has made me think and look at myself. The whole experience from last year has made me confront my own prejudices." It was brave of him to reveal to the focus group members that he had prejudices and that he was made to confront them. His comments indicated that his reflection provided insights into his values and development as a human being. It is hoped that he will take such insights into his classroom as well.

The sixth and final cycle of the study worked with the play *The Tempest* and used articles, debates and problem-solving activities to engage with issues of race, class, gender and power. At the end of cycle six, an interviewee noted that that she would do more than "focus on the content and methods. I know I need to ask; how do I make a difference to their lives?" Another said, "There is always some way to make a difference. I would feel guilty if I let it pass," and another noted that she "didn't want to dwell on change in learners' lives but once you are aware, you can't avoid it." What the comments indicated is that they were willing to confront issues of transformation, and the engagement with the text was making a difference to their own lives.

Finally, an interviewee pointed out that she would use issues that emerged from the texts to help learners develop academically and socially, but noted that "I won't preach. They must make decisions, and apply it to their own lives. It must be theirs." She continued later in the interview, "If I preach to them, I am oppressing them." In many ways, her comments indicated that she understood the complexities of a critical pedagogy approach. While she knew that she was obliged to empower her learners and affirm their lives (Giroux, 2009), she was equally aware that she had to reflect on her practices so that she did not impose her power and advantage on her learners (Habermas, 1972).

Concluding Thoughts

By the end of the study, students understood the importance of having a strong command of subject knowledge, pedagogical skills and a commitment to change, as urged by Freire (2009). They also recognized the importance of teaching with a humanizing pedagogy in an environment characterized by respect (Bartolome, 2009). While their roles and identities will evolve with time and experiences, it is hoped that the knowledge, skills and abilities they have garnered will remain to serve as guiding parameters as they traverse their educational contexts.

References

Anstey, M., & Bull, G. (2006). *Teaching and learning multiliteracies: Changing times, changing literacies*. Newark: International Reading Association.

Apple, M. W. (1989). American realities: Poverty, economy and education. In L. Weis, E. Farrar, & H. Petrie (Eds.), *Dropouts from school* (pp. 205–223). Albany: State University of New York Press.

Bartolome, L. (2009). Beyond the methods fetish: Towards a humanising pedagogy. In A. Darder, M. P. Baltodano, & R. D. Torres (Eds.), *The critical pedagogy reader* (pp. 338–356). New York: Routledge.

Boler, M. (2004). *Democratic dialogue in education: Troubling speech, disturbing silence*. New York: Peter Lang Publishing.

Branagh, K., Evans, S., Parfitt, D. (Producers), & Branagh, K. (Director). (1993). *Much Ado about nothing* [Motion Picture]. United Kingdom & United States of America: Renaissance Films, American Playhouse Theatrical Films & BBC Films.

Ciardiello, A. V. (2004). Democracy's young heroes: An institutional model of critical literacy practices. *The Reading Teacher, 58*(2), 138–147.

Darder, A., Baltodano, M. P., & Torres, R. D. (Eds.). (2009). *The critical pedagogy reader*. New York: Routledge.

Freire, P. (1999). *Pedagogy of hope*. New York: Continuum Publishing Company.

Freire, P. (2009). From pedagogy of the oppressed. In A. Darder, M. P. Baltodano, & R. D. Torres (Eds.), *The critical pedagogy reader* (pp. 52–60). New York: Routledge.

Giroux, H. (1988). *Teachers as intellectuals: Towards a critical pedagogy of learning*. MA: Bergin and Garvey.

Giroux, H. (2009). Teacher education and democratic schooling. In A. Darder, M. P. Baltodano, & R. D. Torres (Eds.), *The critical pedagogy reader* (pp. 438–459). New York: Routledge.

Giroux, H. A., & McLaren, P. (1996). Teacher education and the politics of engagement: The case for democratic schooling. In P. Leistyna, A. Woodrum, & S. A. Sherblom (Eds.), *Breaking free: The transformative power of critical pedagogy* (pp. 301–331). Cambridge: Harvard Educational Review.

Habermas, J. (1972). *Knowledge and human interests*. London: Heinemann.

Henning, S. D. (1993). The integration of language, literature, and culture: Goals and curriculum design. *ADFL Bulletin, 24*(2), 51–55.

Hooks, B. (2009). Confronting class in the classroom. In A. Darder, M. P. Baltodano, & R. D. Torres (Eds.), *The critical pedagogy reader* (pp. 142–150). New York: Routledge.

Johnson, H. and Freedman, L. (2005). *Developing critical awareness at the middle level*. Newark, DE: International Reading Association.

Kudlick, C. (1999). History as (Improv) theatre: Tips for discussion sessions. *Perspectives*. Retrieved February 20, 2009, from www.historians.org

Majidi, M. (1999). *The Colour of Paradise*. Retrieved from https://m.imdb.com<title

McLaren, P. (2009). Critical pedagogy: A look at the major concepts. In A. Darder, M. P. Baltodano, & R. D. Torres (Eds.), *The critical pedagogy reader* (pp. 61–83). New York: Routledge.

Mda, Z. (2002). *The Madonna of Excelsior*. Cape Town: Oxford University Press.

Patton, M. Q. (2002). *Qualitative research & evaluation methods*. Thousand Oaks, CA: Sage Publications, Inc.

Reason, P., & Bradbury, H. (2006). *Handbook of action research: Participative inquiry and practice*. Thousand Oaks, CA: Sage Publications, Inc.

Roy, A. (1997). *The God of small things*. London: Flamingo.

Shakespeare, W. (1913). *The Tempest*. Cape Town: Juta and Company.

The Junction Avenue Theatre Company. (1988). *Sophiatown*. Johannesburg: David Philip Publishers.

8 Academic Development at the Durban University of Technology

Advancing the Transformation Agenda in Higher Education

Thengani Harold Ngwenya

Introduction

Relying on Critical Theory as both a conceptual and analytical framework, this chapter examines the strategic organizational development initiatives of the Durban University of Technology (DUT), with reference to the current and future role of the university's academic development division in advancing the institution's social justice agenda as articulated in its current strategic plan (DUT, 2017). In a theory-informed discussion of academic development/educational development, the chapter locates the vision and goals of the DUT academic development division—known as the Centre for Excellence in Learning and Teaching (CELT)—in the broader context of academic development both in South Africa and globally.

The chapter takes as its point of departure the national legislative and regulatory policy framework, which is underpinned by two often incompatible drivers: national development and global competitiveness. Much of this chapter looks at the transformation of higher education (HE) in the country dating back to the publication in 1997 of the Education *White Paper 3: A Programme for the Transformation of Higher Education* (DoE, 1997) through to the *White Paper on Post-School Education and Training* published in 2013 (DHET).

In the South African context, both at the national and higher education institutional levels, academic development is highly policy driven—primarily by government redistributive policies. Its key activities are informed on the one hand by notions of social justice, equity and redress, and on the other, by the need for South African universities to be globally competitive by producing graduates that can hold their own in the rapidly changing global labor market. Consequently, policy implementation in the South African higher education system may best be characterized as a national development–global competitiveness balancing act. The former requires universities to pay particular attention to issues of social inequality, poverty and unemployment and how these issues could be addressed through critical and responsive policies and institutional development initiatives; the latter emphasizes performance, metrics and compliance. Predictably, the need for global competitiveness has led to the emergence of a market-related discourse in the governance and management of the South African higher education system. As part of the public service, South African universities have had to succumb to what is often presented as the inevitable hegemony of New Public Management (NPM) (Ferlie, Pettigrew, Ashburner, & Fitzgerald, 2006), with its obsession with performance data, outcomes, productivity and endless audits at the expense of developmental processes that are responsive to the country's well-known socio-economic challenges.

The DUT Context

While the DUT Strategic Plan is very much particular to DUT as a university of technology, it seeks to respond to the challenges that characterize universities in this era of (hyper) complexity that has in many ways superseded both postmodernity and the information age. The strategic plan revolves around two themes: student-centeredness and engagement. The four strategic focus areas of the strategic plan seek to create opportunities for fundamental organizational change that will in turn foster the emergence of a student-centered institutional culture as well as various forms of "engagement" within and outside the university. Within this broad institutional context, academic development is positioned to play a pivotal role in the redesign of the curriculum, student and staff development, and academic policy development. Significantly, there is a striking thematic resonance between the strategic priorities of DUT and the following definition of academic development as provided by the country's Council on Higher Education (CHE):

> A field of research and practice that aims to enhance the quality and effectiveness of teaching and learning in higher education, and to enable institutions and the higher education system to meet key educational goals, particularly in relation to equity of access and outcomes. Academic development encompasses four interlinked areas of work: student development (particularly foundational and skills-oriented provision), staff development, curriculum development and institutional development.
>
> (2007, p. 74)

The related DUT strategic focus areas are as follows:

1. Building sustainable student communities of living and learning.
2. Building research and innovation and development.

3. Building a learning organization.
4. Building a sustainable university.

Within the context outlined above, this chapter explores academic development initiatives that, relying on the available expertise and resources in CELT, contribute direct or indirectly to the practical implementation of the strategic focus areas. Given the inherently complex and dynamic nature of universities, it would be imprudent to expect academic development projects and initiatives to deal with all strategic priorities in a mechanistic, formulaic or linear fashion. The aim is to show how the current and planned academic development projects are contributing or are likely to contribute to the transformation and social justice agenda of the university.

The conception of the envisaged transformation is most cogently expressed in the recent *Ministerial Statement on the Implementation of the University Capacity Development Programme through Effective Management and Utilisation of the University Capacity Development Grant 2018–2020*:

> . . . We face a critical juncture in the history of university education in South Africa, and the recent student protests attest to this. Whilst the issue of student funding has been foregrounded in the protests, there are a range of associated issues that have been highlighted but have not received the same level of coverage as the funding issue. This includes issues such as whose participation is being privileged in HE, whose worldviews are being privileged in higher education, and who is experiencing success in the system. The system has been strongly criticized for the slow pace of transformation it has undergone, despite the issue being strongly foregrounded in the range of policy documents since 1994.
>
> (DHET, 2017, p. 2)

Critical Theory as a Conceptual Framework

Critical Theory has a long and varied history but is essentially concerned with issues of social justice, emancipatory knowledge and power relations; as such, it provides the requisite theoretical framework for an emancipatory social science (Wright, 2010). Echoing Jürgen Habermas, Erik Olin Wright, the author of *Envisioning Real Utopias* (2010), described an emancipatory social science in the following terms:

> . . . any emancipatory social science faces three basic tasks: elaborating a systematic diagnosis and critique of the world as it exists; envisioning viable alternatives; and understanding the obstacles, possibilities, and dilemmas of transformation. In different times and different places one

or another of these may be more pressing than others, but all are necessary for a comprehensive emancipatory theory.

(2010, p. 10)

As evidenced by the 2015–16 student protests, the South African HE system
has reached a point where the country's universities need to start "understanding the obstacles, possibilities, and dilemmas of transformation." Academic
developers, as critical educators, have an important role to play in creating
conditions for the fundamental transformation of HE curricula, epistemolo-
gies and approaches to pedagogy (Hytten, 2014).

Critical Theory emerged as a critique of ideas associated with the Enlight-
enment and of the dominance of the positivism, empiricism and reductionism
characterizing the major meta-theoretical approaches to the acquisition of
knowledge, especially in the field of natural sciences. According to Critical
Theorists, positivism had the effect of valorizing scientific facts and, in the
process, underplaying the significance of the socio-historical and political
contexts in which knowledge was produced and disseminated. A collection
of essays titled *The Critical Pedagogy Reader* (Darder, Baltodan, & Torres,
2009, pp. 28–29) captures the main ideas informing the seminal research and
publications of critical theorists associated with the Frankfurt School:

> The Frankfurt School took as one of its central values a commitment to
> penetrate the world of objective appearances to expose the underlying
> social relationships they often conceal. In other words, penetrating such
> appearances meant exposing through critical analysis social relation-
> ships that took on the status of things or objects. For instance, by exam-
> ining notions such as money, consumption, distribution, and production,
> it becomes clear that none of these represents any objective thing or
> fact, but rather all are historically contingent contexts mediated by rela-
> tionships of domination and subordination. In adopting such a perspec-
> tive, the Frankfurt School not only broke with forms of rationality that
> wedded science and technology into new forms of domination, it also
> rejected all forms that subordinated human consciousness and action to
> the imperatives of universal laws.

There are many ways in which Critical Theory could be used in the context
of academic development in a University of Technology. For the purposes of
this chapter it is the emancipatory potential and the foregrounding of social
critique that have a direct resonance with the strategic directions of DUT.
The major focus of the work of academic development practitioners based
in CELT and in the six faculties of the university is the implementation of
practical strategies aimed at enhancing student success—and these practical

strategies, being underpinned by Critical Theory, are thus also transformative. DUT's understanding of student success has discernible thematic affinities with that of the CHE as articulated in the Quality Enhancement Project (QEP), in terms of which student success denotes "Enhanced student learning with a view to increasing the number of graduates with attributes that are personally, professionally and socially valuable" (2014, p. ii). The idea of an all-embracing and inherently educative student experience permeates all the strategic directions of the university, as evident in DUT's strategic plan (2015, p. 5).

Academic development practitioners have always seen themselves as intellectual activists who promote, among other things, a critical approach to the sociology of knowledge and thus favor inherently transformative approaches to their work. It is these approaches that CELT seeks to promote in its contribution to the advancement of both the institutional and national transformation agendas. Writing in 2010, Crain Soudien attempted to provide a broad framework for conceptualizing the meaning of transformation in the HE context:

> There are basically two main approaches to the question: the first sees transformation as a demographic intervention around the imbalances of race, class, gender, language, while the second argues that it is about the nature of privilege and power. . . . The second position argues that transformation is an ideological process which has to engage with domination and its attendant forces and discourses. This position emphasises the distribution of political and economic power in society and the process through which social inclusion and exclusion are effected.
>
> (Soudien, 2010, p. 4)

This second approach to HE transformation is underpinned by Critical Theory, in which the curriculum and its delivery are seen as being patently insidiously political. The idea advanced in this chapter is that uncovering the political nature of the curriculum and promoting the pedagogy of transformation could be led by academic development practitioners; it is no accident that academic development practitioners are also known as curriculum developers (Luckett & Shay, 2017).

Academic Development (AD): National and Global Perspectives

For a variety of complex but interrelated reasons, academic development has increasingly taken center stage in debates about tertiary education in South Africa (Boughey, 2010, Quinn, 2012). The prominence accorded to academic development is evidenced by the fact that a number of South African universities have properly staffed academic development units under the leadership of a director, senior or executive director, or deputy vice chancellor (teaching and learning). Recently, the CHE has given further impetus to this drive to improve teaching and learning through its Quality Enhancement Project. The reasons for this enhanced awareness of the importance of academic development include massification or increased access to tertiary education by students from historically marginalized communities; the rapidly changing nature of what counts as knowledge in the 21st century; the growing realization that university students *need to be taught how to learn* if they are to be lifelong learners and critical thinkers; the changing expectations of employers regarding the attributes of graduates; and the reality of underprepared (especially in the area of higher education pedagogy) lecturers and professors.

Needless to say, the above list is not exhaustive; but it is a clear indication that the higher education system requires a radical reappraisal on a number of fronts if it is to maintain its relevance in the era of the fourth industrial revolution (Schwab, 2017). For instance, there is a growing need to design strategies that would enhance the pedagogical competencies of university teachers as facilitators of learning as well as independent, critical and creative thinking. In the past, the focus has been on disciplinary and in some cases professional expertise, usually evaluated in terms of possession of the appropriate doctoral degree and evidence of being a productive researcher. There is growing recognition, however, that university lecturers need more than advanced training in their disciplines in order to engage in effective teaching, advising, mentoring and assessment in the swiftly changing tertiary education sector.

Renowned Stanford University educational psychologist Lee Shulman (1987) has over the past five decades published incisive articles on teaching in which he argues that teachers (including university teachers, of course) must be equipped with both a mastery of subject or discipline content and pedagogical knowledge; that is, disciplinary knowledge and expertise need to be complemented with a complex repertoire of pedagogical knowledge and expertise.

Shulman's approach resonates with contemporary approaches to the teaching of academic literacies in HE in which the literacies are conceptualized as sites of socialization or of inducting students into the academic discourses and ways of being and doing that define particular disciplines and professions (Wingate, 2015). Citing Schieffelin & Ochs (1986) and Duff (2007), Wingate made the following point, which university teachers and academic development practitioners can only ignore at their own peril:

> Language socialisation refers to the process in which novices learn the language of a specific community, and become competent members of

that community through the use of the language (Schieffelin & Ochs, 1986). As Duff (2007, p. 311) explains, in this process "experts or more proficient members of a group play a very important role in socializing novices and implicitly or explicitly teaching them to think, feel and act in accordance with the values, ideologies, and traditions of the group."

The importance of language in mediating learning cannot be over-emphasized. It is not fortuitous that, for almost a decade, DUT academic development practitioners have been preoccupied with embedding academic literacies in the disciplinary discourses that define the disciplines and make possible deep or meaningful learning in HE. That is to say, beyond a concern with language in the ordinary sense of the word, academic development practitioners have been concerned with the epistemological and discursive paradigms that shape the theory and practice of teaching and learning in HE.

Academic development is thus a response to a recognized need for HE institutions and the societies they serve to be more inclusive in their attempts to expedite student access to and success in HE. This requires a systematic and thorough reappraisal of both the role of academic development and its place in the HE environment.

While each country has its own context-specific conception of academic development, a number of common features have emerged in the related research and literature (see Table 8.1).

In the South African context the draft policy on Programme Classification Structure has identified academic development activities as involving the following:

a. Improving access through the development of alternative admission systems and admissions testing;
b. Development and improvement of Foundation programmes to improve the knowledge and skills levels of students to better equip them for succeeding in the formal programmes of the institution;
c. Academic Staff development and research capacity development;
d. Course and curriculum development and the development of academic frameworks and models;
e. Implementing strategies to improve teaching and learning efficiency;
f. Providing language and writing skills development programmes;
g. Development of educational technology that enhances instruction;
h. Promoting academic engagement;
i. Academic engagement and Public Service programme development;
j. Research Capacity Development initiatives; and
k. HIV/AIDS integration.

(DHET, 2015, p. 31)

Table 8.1 Typical Educational Development/Academic Development Activities

1) **Teach** courses and workshops for teachers (including postgraduate students, newly appointed and more experienced academics).	5) **Research** student and professional learning and organizational development in higher education.	9) **Contribute** during evaluation of teaching and quality assurance processes.
2) **Consult** teachers and other individuals holding positions such as study directors, heads of departments, deans, etc.	6) **Develop** new supportive teaching and learning structures, e.g., reward systems for good teachers.	10) **Aid** in policy and strategy development, nationally and in institutions and departments.
3) **Participate** in curriculum development processes.	7) **Arrange** teaching and learning conferences.	11) **Support** students' enculturation and their development of study strategies.
4) **Administer** teaching and learning funds.	8) **Assess** pedagogical merits during hiring of new teaching staff and/or promotion.	12) **Secure** personal (i.e. individual staff) professional development opportunities through scholarship, research and professional networks.

Source: Gosling (2006).

National education policies such as these are evidence of the very explicit mandate that government provides to the academic development centers/ divisions of South African universities. Clearly, these centers, as is the case elsewhere in the world, have a key role to play not only in educational development but also in the broader quality and organizational development of universities (Haynes & Stensaker, 2006, p. 7).

And yet the global ascendance of a new managerialism in tertiary education (Deem, Hillyard, & Reed, 2007) brings pressure to bear on those working in academic development centers, and often threatens to undermine the hard-won institutional commitment to a critical and transformative approach. The new buzzwords in tertiary education are "accountability," "measurable outputs," "productivity" and "financial viability." Policy makers are unabashedly linking tertiary education and what is glibly and inappropriately dubbed "skills development" to economic growth. In this recognizably utilitarian and instrumentalist discourse on tertiary education, education has become synonymous with training for employment. This has led to the partial or total marginalization of knowledge for its own sake, and of values and attributes that are not immediately usable or useful in the labor market.

Saleem Badat has offered a nuanced critique of the foregrounding of useful and practical knowledge at the expense of values that sustain ethical and critical citizenship:

> An instrumental approach to higher education which reduces its value to its efficacy for economic growth, and calls that higher education should prioritize professional, vocational and career-focused qualifications and programmes and emphasise "skills development" is to denude it of its considerably wider social value and functions.
>
> (2010, p. 14)

It is this instrumentalist and ostensibly pragmatic discourse that DUT seeks to challenge as it systematically reconfigures its academic offerings both at undergraduate and postgraduate levels. Since 2011, as part of its Curriculum Renewal Project (CRP), the university has embarked on a rigorous review of the curriculum, one of the objectives being to align the curriculum with the Senate-approved DUT Graduate Attributes. It is the stated goal of the institution to produce graduates with the intellectual flexibility and dispositional adaptability necessary for engaging in the workplace of the future, which will, invariably, require the capacity for continuous and contextual learning. The proposed curricula will therefore contain a significant component of General Education (30% of SAQA credits); the General Education themes cover academic literacies as defined above, as well as core "habits of mind" such as critical thinking, effective communication and emotional intelligence. At the risk of stating the obvious, it must be pointed out that academic development practitioners are at the forefront of implementing the new strategic plan, especially those aspects of it relating to the curriculum and its delivery.

Many of the pressures currently experienced in HE are inextricably linked to the changing nature of knowledge itself. For all in HE, whether globally or nationally, the complexity of the sector is being further compounded by the radical (in ways that we have not even begun to grasp) disruption experienced by the generation of students currently at university. As products of a highly technologized, hyper-complex, interconnected and globalized world, these 21st-century students are constantly challenging university educators to review our assumptions about teaching and learning. In a world where information on any conceivable topic has become accessible to any person anywhere with the right technological tools, the notions of numeracy, literacy and innovation acquire new meanings by the day. The major challenge facing us as university educators is to equip these students with the capacities that will enable them to transform information into usable and useful knowledge in a variety of professional, personal and social contexts. The hitherto taken-for-granted notions of knowledge and knowing assume different meanings in an era that has been described as the fourth industrial revolution (Schwab, 2017).

While the twin imperatives of boosting national development and global competitiveness are often experienced as contradictory by South African universities, DUT's response to the global-competitiveness challenge is compatible with the institution's social justice and transformative emphasis, which values in its graduates the capacity for continuous and contextual learning. As stated in the most recent version of the university's strategic plan (2017), the institution foregrounds *entrepreneurship* in its academic offices, acknowledging the related challenges of knowledge production and unemployment. As part of its strategy to support students as potential entrepreneurs, the university is designing special programmes focusing on enhancing entrepreneurship, in addition to emphasizing in all curricula the value of agile and entrepreneurial approaches.

Academic Development at DUT

In the South African context, academics—who, like academics all over the world, in addition to their teaching and assessment responsibilities have research, administrative and community engagement obligations—have to grapple with the consequences of a dysfunctional secondary education system that hardly prepares young people for the challenges of tertiary education. Graeme Bloch (2009) has provided an incisive, well-researched and intellectually nuanced historical overview of the South African schooling system. While the government, civil society and non-governmental organizations have been tackling the fundamental but not irresolvable problems that face our schools in the Black townships and remote rural areas, universities have been under pressure to consolidate their academic development initiatives to ensure that students from these schools benefit from tertiary education. Such interventions typically include well-coordinated extended curriculum programmes that are in line with the principles of the *White Paper for Post-School Education and Training* (DHET, 2013) as well as the all-embracing National Development Plan (National Planning Commission, 2012). The setting up and resourcing of academic development centers as support units and agents of transformation is simultaneously an educational project and a political one.

Chrissie Boughey has provided the following account of the history of academic development South Africa:

> In South Africa, academic development (AD) was introduced into the higher education system in the early 1980s in response to the perceived needs of the then, small number of black students entering historically

white, liberal universities . . . broadly termed Academic Support, Academic Development and Institutional Development, are not distinct from each other and are indicative more of dominant discourses constructing what is appropriate as student support than actual periods of time.

(2010, p. 4)

In this chapter, I argue that we have reached a stage in the evolution of academic development that could be characterized as *transformational discourse underpinned by social justice*. Despite ongoing and often effective academic development initiatives to date, there is a pressing urgency to devise more responsive and innovative ways of teaching in tertiary education. CELT's approach to academic development is an all-embracing one, as evident in the list of its existing student, staff and curriculum development programmes:

1. Training of Peer Tutors, Mentors and Advisors.
2. Residence Educational Programme (REP).
3. First-Year Student Experience (FYSE).
4. Extended Curriculum Programmes (ECPs).
5. Training and development of academics in online teaching and assessment.
6. Training of academics in the use of technology in lecture venues.
7. Management and coordination of the University Capacity Development and the Foundation Grants.
8. Induction of new academic staff.
9. Development of academic policies and guidelines.
10. Hosting of the Annual Academic Literacies and English for Academic Purposes Symposium.
11. Hosting of the Annual Learning, Teaching and Assessment Conference.

In order to achieve its objectives, CELT works closely with faculty management structures, including deans and heads of department as well as faculty-based academic development practitioners. As a 2009 survey showed (Gosling), academic development centers take various forms and perform similar but not necessarily the same functions. CELT has settled on a *hybrid* structure, which aims to strike a reasonable balance between centralization and decentralization in terms of structure and function; there is a relatively small complement of staff at the center, and each of the six faculties has its own academic development practitioners whose responsibilities differ per faculty. The latter is only natural given the inherently different professional and disciplinary identities of programmes housed in each faculty.

The conceptual understanding of the university as a learning organization is implicit in CELT's approaches to academic development, in that all its activities are direct responses to the university's strategic plan while also responding to national projects such as the University Capacity Development Programme (UCDP). Like the university as a whole, CELT is constantly adapting to internal and external factors. This is evident in the role played by CELT in university committees and administrative structures as well as in national organizational structures such as Higher Education Learning and Teaching Association of Southern Africa and the Higher Education Quality Committee. Collaboration and systems thinking characterize all the strategic goals of CELT as an academic development division. The systematic and coordinated creation of collaboration platforms such as the FYSE Advisory Committee and CELT's active involvement in faculty structures such as the Teaching and Learning Committees are examples of CELT's interpretation of the concept of networking. The importance of ongoing collaboration between faculty-based academic development practitioners, quality promotion officers and those staff members based in central divisions such as CELT and the Centre for Quality Promotion and Assurance cannot be over-emphasized. For this collaboration to yield the results of enhancing student success and contributing to graduateness, academic departments under the leadership of heads of department have to forge a complex network of collaboration with the support and administrative units of the university.

CELT contributes in demonstrable and measurable ways to the university's strategic focus area of building research and innovation for development. As an academic development division, CELT initiates and leads scholarly debates about the scholarship of teaching and learning. Over the past five years, through workshops, seminars, symposia and conferences, CELT has initiated a culture of research and innovation in the area of learning, teaching and assessment, and will continue to strengthen this culture. The Annual LTA Symposium is already well known within the academic development community nationally and has featured respected scholars in the field of Higher Education Studies as keynote speakers. The Academic Literacies Symposium inaugurated in 2015 has become a robust forum for the scholarly interrogation of both "signature pedagogies" (Shulman, 2005) and academic literacies. The process of developing sustainable communities of practice (Wenger, 1998) has begun in earnest.

In line with the notion of creating a technologically networked university, these communities of practice already have an online presence in the university's learning management system (*Think Learn Zone*). The notion of the network may also be used metaphorically to refer to the various collaborative activities involving colleagues from various sectors, divisions and department of the university.

As evidenced by its involvement in university community engagement initiatives, CELT also subscribes to the notion of the "ecological university"

(Barnett, 2016)—a concept that resonates with the notion of engagement as outlined in DUT's strategic plan. Ronald Barnett (2016, p. 13) has offered a compelling argument for a university that is responsive to its external environment (acknowledges its interconnectedness with the world, both human and physical; promotes human understanding; widens participation; and improves situations in communities), while ensuring ongoing organizational learning. It our view, DUT is and should continue to be a networked university in the manner described by Barnett.

Conclusion

The chapter has provided a contextualized account of the ways in which a typical academic development center in a university can contribute to institutional and national transformation through the judicious execution of its mandate to continuously support and develop academics and students in the areas of teaching and learning. In this chapter, transformation is not only about equity and equality in relation to race, class and gender; it is an all-embracing response to internal and external (including global) pressures to produce graduates with the requisite knowledge and intellectual flexibility to contribute to the creation of a just and humane global community. The chapter has shown how the adoption of a transformative orientation (Land, 2004) to academic development could contribute to institutional development and innovation.

References

Barnett, R. (2016, July 4–5). *The coming of the ecological university*. Philosophy of Higher Education symposium, Hendon. London: Institute of Education.

Bloch, G. (2009). *The toxic mix: What's wrong with South African schools and how to fix it*. Cape Town: Tafelberg.

Boughey, C. (2010). *Academic development for improved efficiency in the higher education and training system in South Africa*. Paper Commissioned by the Development Bank of Southern Africa.

Council on Higher Education. (2007). *HEQC institutional audits manual 2007*. Pretoria: Council on Higher Education.

Darder, A., Baltodan, M. P., & Torres, R. (Eds). (2009). *The critical pedagogy reader*. New York: Routledge.

Deem, R., Hillyard, S., & Reed, M. (2007). *Knowledge, higher education, and the new managerialism*. Oxford: Oxford University Press.

Department of Education. (1997). *Education white paper 3: A programme for the transformation of higher education*. General notice 1196 of 1997. Pretoria: Department of Education.

Department of Higher Education and Training. (2013, November 20). *White paper for post-school education and training*. Pretoria: Department of Higher Education and Training.

DHET. (2015). *Programme classification structure manual.* HEMIS 002.

DHET. (2017). *Ministerial statement on the implementation of the university capacity development programme through effective management and utilisation of the university capacity development grant 2018–2020.* Pretoria: Department of Higher Education and Training.

Duff, P. (2007). Second language socialization as a sociocultural theory: insights and issues. *Language Teaching, 40*, 309–319.

Durban University of Technology. (2015). *Strategic Plan (2015–2019).* Durban: Durban University of Technology.

Durban University of Technology. (2017). *Strategic Plan 2.0 (2017–2019).* Durban: Durban University of Technology.

Ferlie, E., Pettigrew, A., Ashburner, L., & Fitzgerald, L. (2006). *The new public management in action.* New York: Oxford University Press.

Gosling, D. (2006). *Educational development in 2006.* Report from the Heads of Educational Development Group. Survey of Educational Development Units in the UK.

Haynes, A., & Stensaker, B. (2006). Educational development centres: From educational to organisational development? *Quality Assurance in Education, 14*(1), 7–20.

Hytten, K. (2014). Teaching as and for activism: Challenges and possibilities. *Philosophy of Education Society*, 385–394.

Land, R. (2004). *Educational development: Discourse, identity and practice.* Maidenhead: Society for Research into Higher Education & Open University Press.

Luckett, K., & Shay, S. (2017, July 26). Reframing the curriculum: A transformative approach. *Critical Studies in Education*, 1–16. In Press.

National Planning Commission. (2012). *National development plan 2030: Our future—make it work.* Pretoria: Department The Presidency.

Quinn, L. (Ed.). (2012). R*e-imagining academic staff development: Spaces for disruption.* Stellenbosch: Sun Press.

Scheiffelin, B., & Ochs, E. (1986). Language socialization across cultures. *Studies in the social and cultural foundations of language*, Vol. 3. New York, NY: Cambridge University Press.

Schwab, K. (2017). *The fourth industrial revolution.* New York: Crown Publishing Group.

Shulman, L. S. (1987). Knowledge and teaching: Foundation of the new reform. *Harvard Educational Review, 57*(1), 1–21.

Shulman, L. S. (2005). Signature pedagogies in the professions. *Daedalus, 134*(3), 52–59.

Soudien, C. (2010). *Transformation in higher education: A briefing paper.* Paper commissioned by the Development Bank of Southern Africa.

Wenger, E. (1998). *Communities of practice, learning, meaning and identity.* New York: Cambridge University Press.

Wingate, U. (2015). *Academic literacy and student diversity: The case for inclusive practice.* Bristol: Multilingual Matters.

Wright, E. O. (2010). *Envisioning real utopias.* London and New York: Verso.

Theme 6

Additional Policies, Practices and Initiatives

What additional policies, practices and initiatives would be beneficial in further advancing the transformation of higher education institutions in post-apartheid South Africa?

9 Beyond Epistemology

Ontological Transformation in South African Universities

Lester Brian Shawa

Introduction

In post-apartheid South Africa, universities have engaged with varied trans-formation strategies. This chapter examines practices that would be benefi-cial in further advancing transformation in universities. While transformation in South Africa has broadly been viewed as a process of redressing the apart-heid past through racial and gender dynamics (Govinder, Zondo, & Mak-goba, 2013), I focus on the role of the university in transformation in terms of students' teaching and learning experiences.

Drawing on selected post-apartheid higher education policies and the response by the University of KwaZulu-Natal (UKZN), I show the varied efforts to transform universities in South Africa. I also propound a need for the epistemological dimensions in teaching and learning to be complemented by ontological dimensions in furthering transformation. Epistemological dimensions are those transformative aspects that stress the development of the intellect, while ontological aspects are interested in the nature of being— what students actually become after going through a university experience. I posit that in terms of teaching and learning, epistemological aspects alone lack the rigor to mold graduates that could contribute meaningfully to the demands of social justice. I thus contend that, in order to meaningfully con-tribute to the objectives of a transformed, non-racial, non-sexist and demo-cratic higher education (HE) system as set out in the Education White Paper 3 and related policy documents, epistemological aspects of transformation need to be complemented by ontological dimensions. An ontological dimen-sion, Dall'Alba and Barnacle (2007, p. 688) contend:

> . . . means engaging with being-in-the-world differently. As dedicated learning environments, higher education institutions are ideally situated to do this. Not only can they provide a forum for challenging taken-for-granted assumptions, but also promote ways of being that integrate

knowing, acting and being. Indeed, educational institutions cannot help but promote ways of being . . .

Thus, the integration of ontology and epistemology in university teaching and learning is vital in bringing together ways of knowing, acting and being.

Heidegger's Phenomenological Ontology and HE

Drawing on Heidegger's phenomenological ontology, an ontological dimension means that universities should not only appeal to the intellect but also to the development of a holistic human being. To contribute to meaningful transformation, universities should not only focus on what human beings should know (epistemology) but also on what they *are* and could *become* (ontology). In this way, universities would champion "educational approaches that engage the whole person: what they know, how they act and who they are" (Dall'Alba & Barnacle, 2007, p. 688) in order to advance transformation.

In addition to epistemological efforts, I contend that a phenomenological ontology would demand that university education in South Africa draws on three interrelated practices that talk to what students could become: first, that teaching in universities in South Africa should be conceived as a moral practice aimed at molding citizens with the positive attitudes and dispositions necessary to engage with inequities in society; second, that university education in the country should assist students to critique their taken-for-granted assumptions mainly created by the apartheid past and their current contexts in order to produce graduates who could draw on history and their contexts to make their own world better; and, third, that university education in South Africa should be liberating as exemplified by Heidegger's re-reading of Plato's philosophy, especially the allegory of the cave that helps us conceive an understanding of university graduates as liberators of themselves and others. In this way, graduates would not only be knowledgeable about their subject matter, but would also become morally upright, critical of their environment and concerned about the wellbeing of others—attributes pertinent to transformation in South Africa.

Conceptualizing Transformation in South African Universities

While transformation in HE institutions in South Africa has been understood differently by different groups, the common understanding is one that stems from the need to redress past inequalities created by the apartheid regime. As outlined in its Transformation Charter, UKZN has attended to such issues. In their understanding of transformation in HE, Govinder et al. (2013, pp. 1–2) posit:

> At its most basic level, the term "transformation" refers to "a marked change in form, nature or appearance." In the South African context, transformation refers more specifically to change that addresses the imbalances of the past (apartheid) era. It has many facets, including demographic and systemic change.

In many cases, transformation has meant a need to broaden access especially to Black and formerly disadvantaged students, and to recruit more Black South African academics, among others.

There have been some success stories amidst the challenges. For example, Badat (2010) notes the existence of a comprehensive policy agenda, a foundation for a single-coordinated system, increased and broadened participation and gender equity. In terms of teaching and learning, he notes that universities have begun to offer academic programmes that produce high-quality graduates with knowledge, competencies and skills to practice occupations and professions locally and anywhere in the world.

However, the recent student protests—#RhodesMustFall and #Fees MustFall—revealed that the challenges of transformation are deep rooted and cannot only be confronted through improved racial and gender dynamics and an epistemological agenda. In his African Voices lecture at University College London on 25 January 2016, Habib argued that these protests revealed three problems: the alienation of Black students from university education, institutional racism and the slow pace of transformation.

Thus, while several efforts to transform the HE sector are evident at both national policies (DoE, 1997; DHET, 2013; MoE, 2002) and institutional levels, more work needs to be done. For example, while improving racial and gender dynamics is important, more meaningful transformation should also include the way students are educated within universities. I now turn to Heidegger's phenomenological ontology and his understanding of the notion of education that is important in imagining a transformative university education that could contribute to what students could become in South Africa.

Heidegger's Phenomenological Ontology and His Understanding of Education

For Heidegger, Plato's notion of *paideia* (education) is a process of discovering a sense of being (Godowski, 2015). He argues that in Plato's view, "the essence of paideia does not consist in merely pouring knowledge into the unprepared soul . . . genuine education leads us back to ourselves, to the place we are, teaches us to dwell there, and transforms us in the process" (Thomson, 2001, p. 254). An education rooted in ontology necessarily transforms human beings and is an integral part of conceiving transformation in South African universities.

The separation of ontology and epistemology is thus worrying as it has resulted in compartmentalized university education. Thomson (2001) contends that, for Heidegger, the compartmentalization of education has led to notions of instrumentalization, professionalization, vocationalization, corporatization and technologization of the modern university. Dall'Alba and Barnacle (2007) refer to such compartmentalization as hyper-specialization that has led to a focus on epistemology rather than learning in HE.

Heidegger's phenomenological ontology is thus useful in understanding that HE ought to be more than just pouring knowledge into students' minds and should instead touch the whole human being based on the person's lived experiences taking into consideration time, history and context. Applied to transformation, knowledge alone is not enough, as what students actually become is more important in whether or not they will confront the ills in society. Therefore, I argue that a sound incorporation of ontology and epistemology in HE teaching and learning is needed, which means preparing students to use their history and context to reflect on their situatedness, and critique it for the betterment of society. I now turn to UKZN and its response to the transformation agenda.

The University of KwaZulu-Natal from a Transformation Perspective

The UKZN has taken a very visionary approach to transformation and is responding to the national imperatives of redress in many ways. Its response is reflected at two levels, policies and academic programmes that aim to assist both students and staff. Before engaging with my point on the need to consider the ontological dimension in furthering transformation efforts, I briefly explain some of the strides made by UKZN. It is important to note that this is not an exhaustive discussion of all the university's transformation efforts.

Policy Level Transformation Initiatives

The UKZN's vision to be a premier university of African Scholarship is an effort to contribute to the transformation of this institution. In its transformation charter, UKZN regards transformation as deeper and broader than the narrow categorization based on race and gender representation (The UKZN Transformation Charter, n.d.). Transformation is viewed as one way of changing the identity and culture of the university to genuinely reflect its mission. The charter covers six themes: research, teaching, learning and scholarship as a vocation to all; race and gender representation to be evident in all structures; a socially cohesive and inclusive institutional culture thrives; good modes of governance are enshrined; the right to freedom of expression is guaranteed; and advancement of the transformation agenda is said to be the responsibility of all. I briefly make reference to them in turn.

Research, Teaching, Learning and Scholarship as a Vocation to All

According to the university's transformation charter (pp. 12–13), to achieve this theme, a number of aspects are prioritized, including on-going access to learning in order to advance social transformation and redress; freedom of inquiry and research for scholars; globally competitive research and scholarship; socially and contextually relevant research and curricula; the promotion of African languages for scholarship; and reliance on student-centered pedagogies as well as a holistic approach to education—characterized by excellence in teaching and learning to produce skilled, self-confident and socially responsible graduates, who are conscious of their role in contributing to the national development effort and social transformation. The latter is very pertinent to the idea of phenomenological ontology or what students could become.

Race and Gender Representation to be Evident in all Structures

The transformation charter (pp. 14–15) outlines five ways of dealing with race and gender representation within the university. The university seeks to ensure that the staff profile represents the demographics of the province and country and to achieve gender equity at management level. To demonstrate its commitment to transformation, employment equity has become part of the performance management requirements of all line managers. Furthermore, the charter notes that mentoring programmes that develop, support and nurture Black and female academic staff are provided. This is in line with national policy imperatives and is pertinent to transformation.

A Socially Cohesive and Inclusive Institutional Culture Thrives

A socially cohesive and inclusive institutional culture is underscored in the transformation charter (pp. 15–16) that notes that every member of the university community has a responsibility to promote social interaction at the institution. The university provides an enabling policy environment to eliminate all forms of discrimination. Such efforts are important but could be better achieved with the application of the ontological dimensions already alluded to.

Good Modes of Governance Are Enshrined

The transformation charter shows commitment to aspects of good governance that embrace democratic representation, consultation, devolution, accountability and transparency. University leadership is called upon to create an enabling environment that supports good governance.

The Right to Freedom of Expression Is Guaranteed

To sustain transformation, the university charter (pp. 18–19), spells out the need for all within the university community to have the right to be heard.

Advancement of the Transformation Agenda as the Responsibility of All

The charter (pp. 20–21) advances the need for all to take responsibility for the advancement of the transformation agenda.

The transformation charter thus gives direction to transformation that goes beyond the conceptualization of race and gender. For this to be supported further, there is a need to consider ontological dimensions within the teaching and learning role of the university. Apart from the transformation charter, UKZN has carefully designed other institutional policies that contribute to transformation. For example, principle 2 of the UKZN policy on Teaching and Learning (UKZN, 2012) stipulates the need for teaching and learning to respond to the national imperatives of redress and success. Similarly, the UKZN Language Policy (UKZN, 2014) supports the central function of the university, which is to generate and impart knowledge including African indigenous knowledge systems. I now briefly discuss programme level transformation initiatives.

Programme Level Transformation Initiatives

The university has launched several programmes to address the issue of redress. These include access and mentorship programmes, the Writing Place, Come Write with Me and the staff development and induction programmes. I briefly explain these in turn.

Access Programmes

The access programmes developed by the university aim to support disadvantaged students. For example, the Humanities Access Programme engages with students from disadvantaged educational backgrounds to develop their academic and psycho-social skills and enable them to succeed (see http://cohtlu.ukzn.ac.za/access-programme.aspx). Similarly, the Centre for Science Access (CSA) aims to redress inequities among students in the natural and applied sciences (see http://csa.ukzn.ac.za/Homepage.aspx).

Mentorship Programmes

Mentorship programmes are developed to enhance students' academic performance and quick and successful socio-academic integration in the university environment (see http://cohtlu.ukzn.ac.za/mentorship-and-ams-programmes/about.aspx). They help students to understand the demands of the academy.

Academic Monitoring and Support Programmes

Academic monitoring and support programmes are an important transformation tool. They assist students that are categorized as "at risk" academically and thus enable those from disadvantaged educational backgrounds to realize their academic potential (see http://cohtlu.ukzn.ac.za/mentorship-and-ams-programmes/about.aspx).

Writing Place

The Writing Place provides academic support in terms of writing and developing students' critical thinking skills. The programme touches on essay writing and the introduction and understanding of academic concepts (see http://cohtlu.ukzn.ac.za/writing-place.aspx).

Come Write With Me

This programme assists academics to conduct research and publish. Emer-ging authors are mentored by a group of writing mentors over a period of time. The programme contributes to the transformation of the university by promoting research and scholarship (see http://utlo.ukzn.ac.za/CWWM/About ComeWriteWithMe.aspx).

The University Education Induction Programme for Established and New Staff

The university education induction programme is compulsory for all new academic employees and those currently at lecturer level and below. It aims to equip lecturers with knowledge and skills to design and evaluate curricula in HE, design teaching and learning, assess learning in HE and to supervise research in the HE context. The programme thus introduces academics, most of whom have no teacher training, to the pedagogy and scholarship of HE (see http://hes.ukzn.ac.za/StaffInduction.aspx). I now turn to ontological practices that would further advance transformation in South African universities.

Proposed Ontological Initiatives for Transformation in South African Universities

Having examined the different dimensions of efforts to achieve transformation in South African HE institutions from both national and institutional perspectives using UKZN as an example, I now propose further practices to enhance transformation in the country's universities. In terms of teaching and learning, there is a need to complement epistemological efforts with ontological dimensions. I contend that a phenomenological ontology would demand that: teaching in universities in South Africa be conceived as a moral practice aimed at molding citizens with positive attitudes and dispositions necessary to engage with inequities in society; university education in the country should assist students to critique taken-for-granted assumptions mainly created by apartheid and their current contexts in order to produce graduates who can draw on history and their contexts to make their own world better; and that university education in South Africa should be liberating as exemplified by Heidegger's re-reading of Plato's allegory of the cave that promotes an understanding of university graduates as liberators of themselves and others. I discuss these proposals in turn.

Teaching as a Moral Practice in South African Universities

In regarding teaching as a moral practice, universities will be contributing to what students could become by complementing the epistemological aspect with a sense of being. The importance of moral issues is well captured by Osguthorpe (2013, p. 25), who contends that, ". . . the mentor teacher's worries might initially be voiced as a concern about instructional method, but they often are more closely connected to a concern about student teachers' way of being and moral disposition." He adds that such dispositions include the student teacher's level of responsibility, commitment, open-mindedness, care, kindness, politeness and other attributes. These dispositions and attitudes are important in the development of the whole person.

In advancing a transformation agenda, all programmes and courses offered in universities, whether to previously disadvantaged groups or to the general student population, should be presented with a moral orientation, where students are socialized into the attitudes and dispositions necessary to challenge injustices in societies. Academics thus have the responsibility to create responsible citizens.

Academics could assist in making teaching a moral practice in many ways: showing respect in engaging with students; employing deliberative democracy in the classroom that helps to develop respect and listening and sustains debate (Samuelsson, 2016) and using teaching methods such as group work and co-operative and collaborative learning that allows for constructive interaction among students through which they learn the necessary attitudes and dispositions. Making the university teaching process a moral practice is thus useful in molding the whole human being in knowing, acting and being.

Critiquing Taken-for-Granted Assumptions

Heidegger's phenomenological ontology views human beings as capable of becoming and thus always learning and re-learning drawing on their lived experiences and contexts. Lived experiences form part of human beings' taken-for-granted assumptions, which may be a result of distortions (Carr & Kemmis, 1986). Thus, university education should aim to assist students to critique their standpoints that stem from their taken-for-granted assumptions.

The apartheid regime presented a distorted reality to both the majority Black and minority White populations. It instilled a sense of inferiority among Black people and one of superiority among Whites. In the democratic South Africa, universities need to engage with such distortions by designing programmes and courses that allow for genuine conversations aimed at understanding the dignity of all human beings in the social fabric.

Education for Liberation in South African Universities— Heidegger's Re-reading of Plato's Allegory of the Cave

Education for transformation in South Africa could be conceived as a liberating one that helps people to remove the chains of apartheid as exemplified by Plato's allegory of the cave (see https://web.stanford.edu/class/ihum40/cave.pdf). This allegory provides a means to discuss oppressive systems such as apartheid and other hegemonic regimes (Godowski, 2015). I present the allegory in four stages as elaborated in the *Republic*:

Stage One: The Cave and the Fire

Human beings are tied up and imprisoned in a cave. There is a fire behind them and a wall between the fire and the prisoners. People are passing along this wall and all the prisoners in the cave can see by the light of the fire their shadows and what they are carrying.

Stage Two: Freedom

A prisoner is freed and sees the real objects that caused the shadows but he finds it difficult to reconcile the new reality with what he was used to—the reality of shadows.

Stage Three

The freed man slowly gets used to the new reality and begins to understand objects as they really are.

Stage Four

The freed prisoner goes back to the cave to share this newly acquired truth and thus, tries to share his experience with the remaining prisoners. This constitutes the liberation process.

For Rodger and Naughton (2015, p. 950), in stage one human beings are viewed as mere receivers of the world's images with no capacity to question, while in stage two they are seen as failing to understand the new reality and thus take time to interpret it. In stage three, after practicing, human beings now begin to understand the new reality, while in stage four they have convinced of the truth and thus liberated. They then return to the cave where they liberate others.

The cave represents the hegemonic systems that control citizens, and the shadows are the social constructions reflected in that system created by colonizers and the hegemony (Godowski, 2015). In South Africa, the apartheid regime could be likened to the cave and the social constructs around racism to shadows. It can be argued that the apartheid government used its powers of reason instrumentally. The phrase instrumental reasoning, coined by Horkheimer, means purposive reason, more oriented to means to the exclusion of ends (Rasmussen, 2004). It thus explains the power of reason for social control (Habermas, 1984; see Shawa, 2011). Universities in South Africa should guard against perpetuating instrumental reasoning and help students to critique such distortions for the sake of a better South Africa. An ontological education should thus not only challenge the constructs surrounding apartheid but also assist students to be agents of change that are ready to liberate others. Programmes and courses at universities should engender a desire to bring about change in students. This means that there is a need for critical methodologies that help to uncover injustices in society. Such methodologies should help to question issues that deal with social, cultural and economic capitals and assist the university to avoid reproducing the injustices in South Africa.

Conclusion

This chapter focused on furthering transformation through the university's role of teaching and learning in South Africa. While noting transformation efforts at national HE and institutional levels, I argued for the need to complement epistemological dimensions in teaching and learning with ontological aspects. My major argument is that epistemological dimensions alone lack the rigor to contribute to meaningful transformation. Three practices anchored on Heidegger's phenomenological ontology were proposed to effectively contribute to transformation: 1) teaching in South African universities should be viewed as a moral practice; 2) universities need to assist students to critique their taken-for-granted assumptions; and 3) university programmes should assist students to be agents of change and liberators of others.

References

Badat, S. (2010). *The challenges of transformation in higher education and training institutions in South Africa*. Paper commissioned by the Development Bank of Southern Africa.

Carr, A., & Kemmis, S. (1986). *Becoming critical: Education, knowledge and action research*. London: The Farmer Press.

Dall'Alba, G., & Barnacle, R. (2007). An ontological turn for higher education. *Studies in Higher Education, 32*(6), 679–691.

Department of Education. (1997). *The education white paper 3: A programme for the transformation of higher education*. Pretoria: Department of Education.

Department of Higher Education and Training. (2013). *White paper for post-school education and training: Building an expanded, effective and integrated post-school system*. Pretoria: Department of Higher Education and Training.

Godowski, J. (2015). Out of the shadows and into the light: Liberation through education. *The Vermont Connection, 32*(8), 50–56.

Govinder, K., Zondo, N., & Makgoba, M. (2013). A new look at demographic transformation for universities in South Africa. *South Africa Journal of Science, 109*(111–112), 1–11.

Habermas. J. (1984). *The theory of communicative action*, Vol. 1. Boston, MA: Beacon Press.

Habib, A. (2016). *Reimagining the South African university and critically analysing the struggle for its realisation.* African Voices Lecture, University College, London.

Ministry of Education. (2002). *Transformation of higher education: A new institutional landscape for higher education.* Pretoria: Ministry of Education.

Osguthorpe, R. (2013). Attending to ethical and moral dispositions in teacher education. *Issues in Teacher Education, 22*(1), 17–28.

Plato (translated by Thomas Sheehan). (n.d.). The allegory of the cave. *Republic VII.* Retrieved July 10, 2017, from https://web.stanford.edu/class/ihum40/cave.pdf

Rasmussen, D. (2004). Critical theory and philosophy. In D. Rasmussen & J. Swindal (Eds.), *Critical theory.* London: Sage Publications, Inc.

Rodger, J., & Naughton, C. (2015). Heidegger's reinscription of paideia in the context of online learning. *Educational Philosophy and Theory, 47*(9), 949–957.

Samuelsson, M. (2016). Education for deliberative democracy. *Democracy and Education, 24*(1), 1–9.

Shawa, L. B. (2011). *Exploring anti-democratic practices in university policy-steerage, management and governance in Malawi: A critical theory perspective* (Unpublished PhD thesis), Victoria University of Wellington, Wellington, New Zealand.

Thomson, I. (2001). Heidegger on ontological education or how we become what we are. *Inquiry, 44*, 243–268.

University of KwaZulu-Natal. (n.d). *Transformation charter.* Durban: University of KwaZulu-Natal.

University of KwaZulu-Natal. (2012). *Policy on teaching and learning.* Durban: University Tecahing and Learning Office.

University of KwaZulu-Natal. (2014). *Language policy.* Durban: University Teaching and Learning Office.

About the Contributors

Zanele Heavy-Girl Dube-Xaba is Lecturer in the discipline of Travel and Tourism in the School of Education at the University of KwaZulu-Natal, located in Durban, South Africa. She lectures in both undergraduate and postgraduate classes. She supervises Honours and Masters Students. Her teaching and research interests are Curriculum and Pedagogy related to Tourism and Tourism Education. She has presented her work at both national and international conferences. She is involved in the Community/Outreach programmes that include The National and Provincial Tourism Expo and on developing the Tourism Educators' Association.

Eunice N. Ivala is Associate Professor and Coordinator of the Educational Technology Unit at the Centre for Innovative Educational Technology at Cape Peninsula University Technology (CPUT) located in Cape Town, South Africa. Her research focus is in ICT-mediated teaching and learning in developing contexts. She has published/co-published over 60 research papers and co-edited/edited two conference proceedings and one book. In 2018, she won an award for excellence in e-Learning from Global Learn Tech for her research impact in changing educational and individuals' practices. Recently, she was a team member in an international digital storytelling project dealing with foreign youth experiences abroad, which was supported by the European Union, and a team leader of the ICT curriculum appraisal of the National Senior Certificate for Adults (NASCA), and institutional coordinator for the Council for Higher Education quality enhancement project in the area of learning environments. She was also a team member in a National Research Fund (NRF)–British Council Workshop Links project on widening access, success and employability, a collaboration between CPUT and University of East London, UK. She holds a BEd Honours degree from the University of Nairobi, Kenya; a MEd degree in Computer-based Education from University of Natal, Durban, South Africa; and a PhD in Culture, Communication and Media Studies from University of KwaZulu Natal, Durban, South Africa.

Maserole Christina Kgari-Masondo is an ordained Pastor, Apostle and Bishop at The People of God Christian Ministries International. She is a lecturer of History, Geography and Social Science at the University of Kwa Zulu Natal; School of Education in Edgewood. Her research interests are in socio-environmental concerns, indigenous knowledge, forced removals, teaching and learning matters and gender issues.

Fumane P. Khanare is the Acting Head of the School of Education Studies, University of the Free State. She is also a Senior Lecturer and Head of Psychology of Education Discipline in the Faculty of Education at the University of the Free State in Bloemfontein, South Africa. Dr. Khanare lectures in both undergraduate and postgraduate classes and is actively involved in the research supervision of Masters and PhD students in the Psychology of Education Discipline. Her scholarship work is in Positive Psychology, with particular emphasis on psychosocial support for teaching and learning, rural education, HIV and AIDS education, asset mapping, as well as explorations of innovative methodologies, especially visual participatory methods as canals towards agency, transformative, enabling teaching and learning environments. She has presented her work at both national and international conferences.

Simon Bhekimuzi Khoza is Associate Professor: Curriculum Studies/Educational Technology and Academic Leader for Research and Higher Degrees at the University of KwaZulu-Natal, in Durban, South Africa. He coordinates different undergraduate and postgraduate programmes, and teaches and supervises postgraduate research in Curriculum Studies and Educational Technology. He has published in local and international journals.

Rita Kizito is the Director of the Centre of Teaching and Learning at the Nelson Mandela Metropolitan University located in Port Elizabeth, South Africa. Her research is primarily focused in the area of Curriculum and Learning Development. She has spent over 37 years in the Education sector, 18 of which have been in Higher Education, and has a keen interest in conducting evaluations. Her research aims to offer a better understanding of learning activity designs, along with how technologies can be used to facilitate meaning-making contexts such as undergraduate science teaching. Dr. Kizito's research is guided by the assumption that meaning-making is a result of interactions (and/or conversations) with others but can be even better mediated through technologies. By focusing on developing an understanding of social and pragmatic nature of conversations and using this understanding to design learning activities that can improve the efficacy of conversation between teachers and learners, her research will contribute to our understanding of how to facilitate meaningful university teaching, on one hand, and to improve teaching and learning practices on the other. To pursue these goals, she invokes approaches from the Learning Sciences and increasingly, from design-based research methodologies. Dr. Kizito is a recipient of the Cyril O. Houle Scholars in Adult and Continuing Education Program and a fellow of the Higher Education Learning and Teaching Association of Southern Africa (Heltasa) TAU Fellowships Programme. An exciting current direction of her work is in spearheading a working group to start a branch of the International Society of the Learning Sciences www. isls.org/.

Suriamurthee Maistry is Professor in the School of Education at the University of KwaZulu-Natal, located in Durban, South Africa. His research interests include the study of higher education pedagogy (including research supervision). He is also involved in a textbook research study in which he supervises PhD candidates. He is a member of the Umalusi Research Forum, and serves on the Assessment Standards Committee of Umalusi. He has also served as a research consultant to Umalusi on the annual NSC post-examination analysis for FET Economics.

Guy R. Mihindou is an articulate professional, experienced in Academic Development, with qualifications in Sciences of Language, Linguistics, Lexicography, and some courses in Information Communication and Technology (ICT). Values driven, conscientious and strategic, Dr. Mihindou thrives on working with individuals, teams and organizations to frame and deliver on objectives through innovative, collaborative and sustainable programmes. Dr. Mihindou holds a BA degree (honors), Linguistic and MA in Science of Languages from Omar Bongo University (UOB) in Gabon and a D Litt in Lexicography from Stellenbosch University, South Africa. He is Head of Department: Academic Development and Innovation (ADI) at the university of Johannesburg (UJ) South Africa. He is a founding member and co-convener of the Academic Development Center (ADC) annual symposium for the last five consecutive years at UJ. The intention of the symposium is fostering collaborative work between ADC and academic staff in faculties and various departments of the University of Johannesburg. He also lectures, moderates and manages the University of Johannesburg English Language programme (UJELP), geared towards the development of International students from non-English-speaking countries seeking to pursue their studies at the university. Dr. Mihindou has been programme director for Business Communication and Writing for Intergovernmental Professionals (BCWIP), a short course designed initially in response to a request by the United Nations Economic Commission for Africa (UNECA) in collaboration with University of Johannesburg International Office (IO) and The United Nations African Institute for Economic Development and Planning (IDEP) in Dakar Senegal.

Ncamisile P. Mthiyane is Lecturer in the Life Orientation Education Department in the School of Education at the University of KwaZulu-Natal, in Durban, South Africa. She lectures in both undergraduate and postgraduate classes. She also supervises Honours, Masters and PhD students in the Psychology of Education Department. She graduated with her BA degree in Psychology and Communication at University of South Africa (UNISA) and obtained her Masters in Psychology of Education at the former University of Durban-Westville. She graduated with her PhD in Educational Psychology in the University of the Free State in 2015. Her research interest areas are adolescents' contextual-based psychosocial issues, innovative and creative strategies in teaching and learning including participatory visual methods in higher education and career guidance and counseling in schools. She has presented her work at both national and international conferences.

Thengani Harold Ngwenya is Professor and the Director of the Centre for Excellence in Learning and Teaching (CELT) at the Durban University of Technology in Durban, South Africa. His research interests include African Literature, Academic Development and Quality Improvement in Higher Education.

Ansurie Pillay is a graduate of the Universities of Durban-Westville and KwaZulu-Natal. She is currently a Senior Lecturer in English Education in the School of Education, University of KwaZulu-Natal in Durban, South Africa where she teaches and supervises students. Her research interests include participatory action research, critical pedagogy, teacher education and change agency, among others. She has been a high school teacher of English and Drama, and a television producer for the SABC and for non-governmental organizations (NGOs). As a television producer, she won a Commonwealth Vision Award in London for excellence in filmmaking. In 2017, Dr. Pillay won the Distinguished Teachers Award from the University of KwaZulu-Natal.

Chaunda L. Scott earned a doctorate in Organizational Leadership with a focus in diversity education from Teachers College/Columbia University in New York City, New York, USA, and a Master of Education degree in the area of Administration, Planning and Social Policy from the Harvard Graduate School of Education in Cambridge, Massachusetts, USA. She is currently an Associate Professor in the Department of Organizational Leadership in the School of Education and Human Services at Oakland University in Rochester, Michigan, USA and Coordinator of the Graduate Human Diversity Inclusion and Social Justice Interdisciplinary Certificate Program. She also serves as the Diversity and Inclusion Specialist for the Office of the Dean in the school. In addition to the above, in 2018, Dr. Scott was selected by the Office of Academic Affairs at Oakland University for a prestigious Special Diversity Assignment. In the Department of Organizational Leadership, she teaches undergraduate and graduate courses focused in the areas of workforce diversity, human resource development, organizational leadership and training and development. Additionally, she supervises diversity and social justice focused dissertations. In the area of scholarship, Dr. Scott has published several national and international diversity education and workforce diversity scholarly articles, book chapters, a book review and four co-edited workforce diversity books. She is also a recipient of an Academy of Human Resource Development's prominent Cutting Edge Research Award, and she has been named as one of the *Top 25 Education Professors in Michigan* by Online Schools. Most notable in 2015, she was granted a prestigious Fulbright Specialist Award that took her to Cape Town, South Africa where she provided professional development seminars at Cape Peninsula University of Technology to administrators and faculty in areas of diversity curriculum and program development. She also received the Educator of the Year Award in 2015 from the Niagara Foundation—Michigan Chapter for her exemplary diversity education work at Oakland University. In 2018, Dr. Scott was recognized at the 23rd Annual Oakland University Faculty Recognition Luncheon for her highly regarded and cutting edge workforce diversity scholarship.

Lester Brian Shawa is Senior Lecturer in Higher Education Studies and coordinator of the Postgraduate Diploma in Higher Education at the University of KwaZulu Natal in Durban, South Africa. His research interests include Higher Education policy praxis (policy, governance and management), Higher Education pedagogy and curricula, and quality discourses in Higher Education.

Index

Note: Page numbers in *italics* indicate figures and page numbers in **bold** indicate tables.

www.ingramcontent.com/pod-product-compliance
Ingram Content Group UK Ltd.
Pitfield, Milton Keynes, MK11 3LW, UK
UKHW020417010325
455677UK00029B/915